M000298468

STRUGGLING READERS

Why Band-aids Don't Stick and Worksheets Don't Work

Lori Jamison Rog

Pembroke Publishers Limited

© 2014 Lori Jamison Rog

Pembroke Publishers
538 Hood Road
Markham, Ontario, Canada L3R 3K9
www.pembrokepublishers.com

Distributed in the U.S. by Stenhouse Publishers
480 Congress Street
Portland, ME 04101
www.stenhouse.com

All rights reserved.
No part of this publication may be reproduced in any form or by any means electronic
or mechanical, including photocopy, scanning, recording, or any information, storage
or retrieval system, without permission in writing from the publisher. Excerpts from
this publication may be reproduced under licence from Access Copyright, or with the
express written permission of Pembroke Publishers Limited, or as permitted by law.

Every effort has been made to contact copyright holders for permission to reproduce
borrowed material. The publishers apologize for any such omissions and will be pleased
to rectify them in subsequent reprints of the book.

We acknowledge the financial support of the Government of Canada through the
Canada Book Fund (CBF) for our publishing activities.

We acknowledge the assistance of the Government of Ontario through the Ontario
Media Development Corporation's Ontario Book Initiative.

Library and Archives Canada Cataloguing in Publication

Rog, Lori, author
  Struggling readers : why band-aids don't stick and worksheets don't work / Lori
Jamison Rog.

Includes bibliographical references and index.
Issued in print and electronic formats.
ISBN 978-1-55138-292-0 (pbk.).--ISBN 978-1-55138-858-8 (pdf)

  1. Guided reading. 2. Reading (Elementary). 3. Reading (Middle school). I. Title.

LB1050.377.R65 2014   372.41'62   C2013-907484-8
                                        C2013-907485-6

Editor: Kat Mototsune
Cover Design: John Zehethofer
Typesetting: Jay Tee Graphics Ltd.

Printed and bound in Canada
9 8 7 6 5 4 3 2 1

MIX
Paper from
responsible sources
FSC® C004071

Contents

Introduction: What Do Struggling Readers Need?

Charlie was one of my most memorable students from the early years of my career. With his ready smile and quick wit, Charlie was popular with both teachers and students. He always had an answer for every question, and whether or not his answers were correct, they were always entertaining. Charlie was the star of the class—except when it came to reading.

Charlie came to school with limited experiences with print. In Kindergarten when the other children were learning their letters, Charlie made towers with the alphabet blocks. In Grade 1 he struggled with letters and sounds but, with lots of help, he managed to crack the code by the end of Grade 2. In Grade 3, when most of his friends were reading chapter books with fluency, Charlie was still sounding out a lot of words, relying on picture cues, and mostly avoiding books whenever he could. When Charlie arrived at my door in Grade 4, he was clearly in trouble. He spent most of the independent reading time at the bookshelf "choosing a book." He carried novels around like props, only pretending to read them. In content-area reading, he was totally out of his depth.

Charlie's problems with reading were not unique to him then, and they're not unique today. The bad news is that, despite the decades of research on reading instruction since I taught Charlie, we've made little progress in reducing the percentage of students who struggle with reading. Most statistics indicate that about a quarter of the students in any grade are reading below grade level. And we are quite likely to have more than one "Charlie" in any classroom. These students are often (but not always) boys. During reading time, they might fake reading, get a friend to read for them, or simply misbehave. After all, most kids would rather get attention for being "bad" than for being "dumb."

Of course, there's no single mold from which all struggling learners are cast. There are many different reasons readers struggle. Medical, cognitive, emotional, and behavioral challenges undoubtedly interfere with learning; these are serious disabilities that are not within the purview of this book. But for most students with reading difficulties, there are a whole range of needs that can—and must—be dealt with by the classroom teacher: students whose first language is not the language of instruction; students whose life experiences do not provide the background knowledge needed to access academic or literary texts; students whose ability or speed of functioning is just a little slower than that of their peers; students who missed picking up some key skills along the way; students who *can* read, but have lost the motivation to do so. These are the "extra scoop" kids—students who often need just a little more teaching or practice or attention to get them on track with reading. And the good news is that it's not too late, even in middle school, to provide those extra scoops of instruction that will get the great majority of these students back on track (Roberts, G. et al, 2013).

We used to assume that by Grade 6 or 7 or 8, reading difficulties were irreversible, and our best option was to provide "band-aid" solutions like week-ahead reading, reading the text aloud to students who couldn't manage it on their own, buddying up struggling readers with more competent readers, or simply s-l-o-w-i-n-g d-o-w-n the whole process. However, the problem with band-aids, as we know, is that they simply don't stick forever. Another outdated school of thought is that struggling readers just need more practice on discrete skills, like decoding and letter patterns. (In truth, only about 10% of struggling adolescent readers have issues with decoding.) So reading class meant lots of time with worksheets and little time with actual reading. As a result, the kids who needed reading practice the most got it the least, a phenomenon sometimes referred to as "the Matthew effect," a Biblical reference to the rich getting richer and the poor getting poorer (Stanovich, 1986).

What struggling readers really need is opportunities to read a lot, with texts that they *can* and *want to* read. They need explicit instruction in the long-term strategies that will enable them to tackle tough texts when a teacher or reading buddy isn't on hand. They need to build, not just competence, but also confidence in themselves as readers, writers, and thinkers. Really, isn't that what *all* readers need? In fact, research has shown that good instruction for struggling readers is not very different from good instruction for students reading at grade level (Torgesen et al, 2007). But struggling readers need that good instruction even more.

This book is about teaching and learning—the explicit instruction, modeling, and demonstration of the habits of effective readers; and routines for guided practice and independent application by students. It is organized around the instructional needs of struggling readers:

- the need for teaching and texts targeted toward their needs
- the need to read more—a lot more
- the need for explicit instruction and guided practice in comprehension strategies
- the need to build vocabulary and fluency
- the need to be able to read informational and functional texts
- the need to use writing to make sense of reading

In the chapters of this book, you will find a range of teaching ideas from which to choose as you plan instruction targeted to the unique needs of your students. Although most of the lesson routines are specifically designed for small-group instruction, they can be easily adapted to whole-class or individualized learning. Each lesson is focused around a specific learning goal and includes a *must-do*— a learning activity that requires students to independently practice what they learned in the lesson.

In my previous book, *Guiding Readers: Making the most of the 18-minute guided reading lesson,* I included just one chapter on small-group reading instruction for struggling readers in upper grades. But I kept hearing from teachers of upper-elementary- and intermediate-grade students that they wanted more lesson routines geared to their grade levels. This book emerged from their requests. Teachers familiar with *Guiding Readers* will recognize some of my favorite material, such as the Reading Toolkit, "clicks and clunks" reading, and the Independent Reading Log—here, they are all carefully chosen to be appropriate for students in Grades 3 to 9.

It's not enough to simply help struggling readers read today's material; they need to build strategic independence to read tomorrow's texts on their own. It's not enough to simply make some progress; we need to *accelerate* progress so they catch up to their grade-level peers before it's too late. And we need real instruction that works, since we know that worksheets simply don't work and band-aids won't stick. This book is intended to provide a collection of practical and proven teaching ideas for anyone working with struggling readers, many of whom just need that "extra scoop" of instruction that will help them become the confident, independent, and strategic readers of tomorrow.

1

Struggling Readers Need Teaching and Texts Targeted to Their Needs

Recently I gave a presentation about struggling readers to a group of teachers. As I expounded on themes of readability, differentiation, reading volume, and the gradual release of responsibility, one participant raised her hand. "But," she asked tentatively, "where do I start?" That's a good question, and one that challenges experienced and novice teachers alike. With rigorous curricula, increasing class sizes, and more and more demands on both teachers and students, it's hard to know how to fit differentiated instruction for struggling readers into the mix.

That's why it's more important than ever to make the most of every minute of instructional time—which means starting with assessment. Once we have assessment data, we can organize our class for instruction, find texts that offer just the right amount of support and challenge to stretch our students, and plan instruction that is targeted to our students' needs and makes the most of valuable teacher time.

> **Where Do We Start?**
> 1. Conduct Assessments: What do my students already know? What do they need to learn?
> 2. Establish Instructional Groups: How can I organize small groups to maximize teaching time and differentiate instruction?
> 3. Select Appropriate Texts: How do I choose texts that engage and support students while stretching their reading abilities to higher levels?
> 4. Plan Instruction: How do I teach students what they need to know, scaffold them as they build their reading strategies and skills, and guide them in applying those strategies independently?

Conducting Assessments

It doesn't take a sophisticated test to tell which students are reading below grade level; we can usually figure that out pretty easily and quickly. What we need to know is *why* these students are not reading at grade level, at what level they *are* reading, and, most importantly, what they need in order to progress from where they are to where they should be. That's why assessment is so important: it enables us to gather information about our students' strengths and needs as readers in order to plan the instruction that is best for them.

There are many different reasons why readers struggle. Some students can read the words but fail to understand the text. Others struggle so much with fluency that it limits both how well and how much they read. Some readers fail to grasp the inferences that enable them to interpret nuances of meaning. Without assessment, we don't know what our students' issues are or what to do about them. Our struggling readers have already fallen behind—sometimes years behind—their peers. It's not enough for instruction to *maintain* growth; it must *accelerate* growth if these students are to catch up. There's simply no time to waste on instruction that doesn't target the specific needs of our students. Using assessment to guide instruction helps us get the most bang for our pedagogical buck.

Most traditional reading assessments consist of a reading passage and comprehension questions: the student reads the passage to him/herself, then writes the answers to the questions. Unfortunately, our struggling readers almost always have trouble expressing themselves in writing, so asking them to write extended responses puts them at an automatic disadvantage.

The best way to determine what our students know and can do is simply to listen to them read and to talk to them about their reading. In an oral reading record (sometimes called a running record or informal reading inventory) the teacher listens to the student read aloud and records the errors, or miscues, made in word accuracy. It's usually accompanied by a comprehension check in the form of questions or retelling (or both), and sometimes by a fluency analysis. This one-on-one time enables the teacher to observe each student's reading behaviors and attitudes, and provides invaluable data about a student's strengths and weaknesses, such as

- Word-level accuracy: What percentage of the words in the passage does the student read automatically? Which words does he/she manage to figure out without help?
- Word-solving strategies: What kinds of strategies does the reader use to solve unknown words?
- Self-correction habits: Does the reader correct his/her own errors? How often do word-level errors interfere with the meaning of the passage?
- Fluency: Does the student read with appropriate speed, phrasing, and expression? Does he/she sound out too many words or pause at inappropriate places?
- Comprehension: Can the reader understand and interpret what is said in the text?
- Strategy use: Is the student able to draw inferences about the text? Can the student explain any strategies he/she used to make sense of the text? Can the student provide evidence from the text to support his/her thinking?
- Reading behaviors: Is the reader engaged or uninterested, calm or nervous, positive or negative about the reading experience? Does he/she frequently hesitate during the reading, repeat phrases, or lose his/her place in the text?
- Reading level: How well does this reader cope with text at a particular level? What levels of texts can he/she read with ease? What can he/she read with support?

Perhaps the most important advantage of the individual assessment is that it enables the teacher to ask the student questions about his/her reading, to probe his/her thinking, and to invite elaboration or explanation from the text in a way that is impossible when grading a pencil-and-paper test.

There's nothing to prevent teachers from gathering reading passages and creating comprehension tasks for their own reading assessments. (The term *running record* comes from the premise that this type of assessment could be done "on the run" with any text.) But time is at a premium for every teacher, and there are many decent published assessments available for purchase. Some features to look for:

- a collection of short passages, graded at several levels of difficulty
- a measure of different elements of comprehension: e.g., locating information in the text, drawing inferences, using vocabulary
- a fluency check
- a place to record reading behaviors and attitudes

See Appendix B: Oral Reading Assessment, for step-by-step instructions on conducting an individual reading assessment.

Graded passages are used to find out what students *can* read, not just what they can't read. Testing struggling readers with grade-level reading material often tells us only what we already know: that they can't cope with grade-level reading material. In order to determine which strategies a reader is using and which strategies need work, we need to find that reader's *instructional* reading level; i.e., the level at which the reading is only a little bit challenging.

Fitting In Individual Assessment

It might seem difficult to justify the time expended in individually testing every reader in your class. But assessment time is educational time. As long as the assessment is providing useful data that informs instruction, it is a good use of class time. An oral reading check takes only about ten minutes. So how can we find that precious ten minutes for each student in our class?

We can take oral reading records during any time other students are engaged in independent work. I find a good opportunity is during daily independent reading time. Each day, while the rest of the students read on their own for 20 minutes or so, I can listen to a couple of students read to me privately. In that way, over two to three weeks, I get to meet with every student. It's not necessary to conduct every student's oral reading record on the same day; spreading out the assessments over a few weeks will still provide reliable information in a manageable way.

Ideally, we want to collect informal oral–reading-record data for each of our struggling readers about once a month; for the remaining students, who are reading at grade level or above, one reading assessment per reporting period is recommended. Some teachers question the need for individual oral reading inventories for students reading at or above grade level. But this assessment can provide valuable information about any student's reading behaviors, and even capable readers can turn into struggling readers if they encounter an unfamiliar task or text form. For example, many teachers report having students who cope quite adequately with narrative texts, but fall apart when confronted with informational texts. And there are always students who benefit from enrichment beyond grade-level reading materials. Ten minutes of one-on-one time with every student each reporting period seems like time well-spent to head problems off at the pass and provide every student with the instruction he/she needs.

Forming Instructional Groups

Assessment also informs us about students with common needs. We can use this information to maximize instructional time by working with students in small groups. Ideally, all the students in the class will experience some small-group instruction; for struggling learners, it's a necessity. Kathy Ganske and her colleagues identify small-group instruction as a critical literacy component for struggling readers, noting that "the small group format enables teachers to more easily maintain the focus and attention of children who may otherwise be disengaged, and it makes it easier for them to monitor behaviors and adjust instruction accordingly" (Ganske et al, 2003: 122). Small-group structures facilitate both targeted teaching and ongoing evaluation of students' progress.

See Chapter 2 for more information on planning small-group instruction.

Research on Response to Intervention (RTI) recommends that struggling readers benefit most from daily support in very small groups of no more than two or three students (Allington, 2009). This level of intervention is difficult for a classroom teacher without additional support, but it should be quite possible to carve 20 minutes a day out of the classroom program to provide targeted intervention for a group of four to six reluctant readers.

Choosing Reading Materials

"The research has clearly demonstrated the need for students to have instructional texts that they can read accurately, fluently, and with good comprehension if we hope to foster academic achievement." Richard Allington (2001: 60))

It's been said that if there's a child who won't read, it only means that he/she hasn't found the right book yet. That might be oversimplifying things, but there *is* something magical about putting the right book in a reader's hands at the right time.

For a book to be "just right" for any of us, we need to be interested, not just in the content, but also in the theme and style. It has to be manageable: too difficult and we'll lose interest; too easy and we'll likely be bored. Finding that just-right text is even more critical for struggling readers, who are usually neither interested in reading nor confident about their ability to do it. So how do we find books these kids are willing—much less want—to read?

Seventy years ago, Emmett Betts (1946) conducted seminal research on text difficulty levels that is still used as a guideline for text selection in classrooms today. Betts defined texts at *independent level* as those for which the reader could process all the words with ease and understand the text completely. He considered that if a reader struggled with as few as 5% of the words or had inadequate comprehension, that text was at the reader's *frustration level*, simply too difficult to read on his/her own without a great deal of support. In between, texts in which a reader could read most of the words easily and demonstrate general comprehension, were deemed to be at the *instructional level* for that reader. This level of text was considered optimal for instruction because it offered enough support for the reader to navigate most of the material, but had enough challenge to require some reading work. It was assumed that there would be some teacher support for reading these texts; hence the use of *instructional*.

We all know that "frustration" is a relative term. The extent of challenge any of us is willing to tackle will vary depending on our interest in the text, our motivation to read it, and our confidence that we will ultimately understand and enjoy it. But the world of frustration-level reading is all too familiar terrain for our struggling readers. By the time they reach our classroom doors, they've already had several years of academic failure and often don't have the confidence in their own abilities to manage tough texts or the stamina to even try. They are afraid of appearing stupid. They might hit frustration at even lower levels than more-capable readers.

All too often, with the best of intentions, we give weak readers the same texts as their grade-level peers, so they won't feel singled out. But research suggests that a steady dose of grade-level text for below–grade-level readers not only fails to help them grow, it can even set them back. A classic study by Carolyn Denham and Anne Lieberman (1980) found that the higher the rates of success with a task, the greater the student learning (not to mention improved attitudes toward learning). Difficult tasks, on the other hand, had a *negative* impact on learning. This was particularly true for struggling learners (Swanson & Hoskyn, 1998). Even the Common Core State Standards document, which advocates increasing the complexity of texts students read, is clear on the subject: "Students need opportunities to stretch their reading abilities but also to experience the satisfaction and pleasure of easy, fluent reading within [their reading abilities]" (Appendix: 9).

An oral reading inventory with a comprehension component will help you select the appropriate level of text for your students. These guidelines might be helpful:

- For *independent reading*, guide students in choosing texts they are interested in and can read with ease.
- For *instruction*, use texts that stretch students just beyond their current reading level.
- If students are required to access texts at their *frustration* level (e.g., content-area text books, or complex literary texts), provide heavy-duty scaffolding or read the text aloud.

Independent-Level Text	*Instructional-Level Text*	*Frustration-Level Text*
98–100% accuracy and thorough (100%) comprehension	95–98% accuracy and adequate (~75%) comprehension	Less than 95% accuracy or inadequate comprehension

"Tiptoe" Texts for Instruction

For most of us, standing on our tiptoes for a while is not too difficult, but every now and then we might need a little support to help us balance. This is, I believe, is an apt metaphor for the kinds of texts we should be using for instruction: texts that students can manage largely on their own, but that present just enough challenge to stretch them as readers and require them to work a little at balance.

Throughout this book, I frequently use the terms *accessible* or *manageable* to refer to texts in which readers are able to read most of the words, navigate the organizational features of the text, and construct meaning from the text *with a little extra effort*. The real craft for teachers is to help students find reading that meets them where they are at the moment, then gradually scaffold them to extend their reach as readers.

Five considerations in making that important reader–text match:

1. Content: Look for themes or topics that match the interests and background knowledge of the reader.

When we understand a bit about readability, the features of a text that make it more or less challenging, and the needs and interests of our students, we are better able to help our students find those just-right texts that will help them grow as readers. For more information about how the science of readability and the art of leveling can guide us in determining the challenges and supports in any text, see Appendix C.

2. Text Structure: Consider the text structure and appearance of the book. Are the text features (i.e., visuals, headings, fonts) likely to support or challenge this reader? Do the line and word spacing, print size, and appearance of the page seem appropriate for the reader's age and stage of development?
3. Concepts and Vocabulary: Skim random pages near the beginning, middle, and end of the book. Do the concepts and vocabulary seem manageable for this reader?
4. Technical Readability: If the text seems appropriate, you might want to do a quick analysis of the technical difficulty. At two or three random points in the book, take a 100-word passage and find the technical readability score.
5. Reader Test: Have the reader read a random page aloud and use a technique such as the High-Five tool (page 29) to judge if the text is appropriate for him/her.

Planning Instruction

This book offers a collection of teaching routines and ideas from which to choose when planning instruction. The lessons in the book are designed for small-group instruction, and they can certainly be adapted to be used with the whole class or with individuals. But each lesson requires your special touch to make it work for your students. In some cases, you will need to provide explicit instruction in the focus strategy or goal. In other cases, the lesson will serve as an opportunity for guided practice. In every case, the small-group instruction will be carefully structured and focused around specific learning goals geared to the needs of the students.

Once you have gathered assessment data, you can go on to plan instruction. The If/Then chart on page 15 identifies a few common reading problems and suggestions for instruction.

If/Then Chart

If...	Then...	Where to Find Support
the student avoids reading whenever possible...	• Provide daily time in class where independent reading practice is expected. • Allow students to choose what they are going to read. • Engage the student in conversations about his/her interests and help him/her find books that match those interests. • Build confidence with easy recreational reading.	Chapter 3
the student lacks adequate background knowledge to access academic and literary texts...	Build and activate background knowledge by • ensuring that students have many opportunities for wide reading • providing text introductions for assigned reading • discussing what background knowledge is necessary for understanding ideas in the text • teaching students how to independently preview texts • reading aloud to students from texts they would not be able to read on their own	Chapters 2, 4, 8
the student chooses books for independent reading that are too difficult or too easy...	• Teach techniques for deciding whether a particular book is too difficult for a reader. • Help him/her find engaging reading materials that stretch him/her just a bit, but not too much. • Relax! Allow him/her to read easy books to build confidence and reading enjoyment.	Chapter 3
the student can read the words, but doesn't remember or understand what he/she has read...	Help him/her move from "word calling" to comprehension by • focusing on reading short chunks of text and retelling • pausing frequently to discuss and analyze reading • encouraging him/her to track thinking with sticky notes • providing graphic organizers that require students to record their thinking as they read	Chapters 5, 10
the student has a basic understanding of what he/she reads, but fails to grasp inferences or read between the lines...	Scaffold him/her in building inference by • providing guided practice with read-aloud texts • making the process of inference more explicit by analyzing clues from the text and background knowledge required • marking pause points in the text for students to stop and record their inferences	Chapter 5
the student doesn't repair comprehension breakdowns and might not even realize when he/she doesn't understand what he/she reads...	Help him/her build strategies for self-monitoring, such as • pausing regularly to consider whether the text is making sense • asking him/herself questions, then anticipating the answers and reading on • making personal connections to the text during reading	Chapter 5

If...	Then...	Where to Find Support
the student offers only literal or superficial responses to reading...	<ul><li>Provide plenty of opportunities for discussion.</li><li>Ask questions that encourage higher-level thinking.</li><li>Encourage students to elaborate on their responses and provide support from the text.</li></ul>	Chapters 4, 10
the student reads very slowly and hesitantly...	Help build fluency by<ul><li>ensuring that the student is reading texts at his/her independent reading level</li><li>providing opportunities for repeated reading of texts, with one-on-one coaching to improve fluency</li><li>providing shared, paired, and choral reading opportunities</li><li>engaging readers in performance reading (e.g., readers theatre) with plenty of time to practice and rehearse</li></ul>	Chapter 7
the student relies too heavily on sounding out words...	<ul><li>Practice automatic word recognition.</li><li>Offer explicit instruction and practice in other word-solving strategies, such as<ul><li>chunking words into segments such as prefixes, roots, and suffixes</li><li>using context clues</li><li>using resources such as dictionaries and pronunciation keys</li></ul></li></ul>	Chapter 6
the student makes miscues that interfere with meaning and doesn't self-correct them...	Help him/her develop a repertoire of self-monitoring strategies, such as<ul><li>pausing frequently to think about whether the reading makes sense</li><li>if it doesn't make sense, stopping and rereading or reading on for clarification</li><li>trying another word that makes sense in the passage.</li><li>applying comprehension and word-solving strategies</li></ul>	Chapters 4, 5, 6
the student has trouble getting the gist of what he/she is reading...	Teach and practice summarizing by<ul><li>asking students to retell, then teaching them to consolidate details into a summary</li><li>having students use sticky notes to mark key ideas in a text</li><li>using graphic organizers to record main ideas and supporting details</li></ul>	Chapters 4, 10
the student offers weak written responses to reading...	Establish expectations that ideas, opinions, and responses must be supported with evidence from the text by<ul><li>teaching students to always explain *why*, even if it is not asked</li><li>practicing scanning the text for specific details</li></ul>	Chapter 10

2

Struggling Readers Need to Learn in Small Groups

One size doesn't fit all, in reading instruction or running shoes. The evidence is clear: when struggling readers are subjected exclusively to the same instruction as the rest of the class, they not only fail to grow, but can actually backslide in their reading proficiency and attitudes (Allington, 2009). In a study of 120 students who received only whole-class instruction with grade-level texts for an entire year, the high-achieving students made a full year's progress, but low achievers gained only three months (Vaughn et al, 2000).

Certainly, there's a place for whole-class instruction—for explaining new concepts or introducing unfamiliar text forms—as long as the learning goals are appropriate for all the students in the class. For example, we need to expose students at every level to fluent, expressive read-alouds of complex texts that they might not be able to read on their own. We need to provide plenty of opportunities for all students to read independently for extended periods of time. But somewhere between reading *to* students and reading *by* students, there must be a place for reading *with* students—an opportunity for students to receive differentiated support in the concepts and strategies they have been taught. That's where small-group instruction comes in.

No doubt you're already thinking, *Comprehension strategies, reader response, sustained silent reading, shared reading, read-aloud, oral language development, listening skills, grammar instruction, word-solving tools, fluency, writing workshop...oh, and let's not forget that special assembly and the fire drill. And now you're telling me to add small-group instruction? How can I possibly fit all that into our literacy block? It's like trying to fit size 9 feet into size 7 Nikes.* If so, you're not alone. A study of 191 teachers from across the U.S. listed time, organization, and classroom management among the top concerns of teachers dealing with struggling readers (Ganske, Monroe, & Strickland, 2003).

Ideally, all of our students should have opportunities for small-group instruction; this experience is particularly critical for struggling readers. At the very least, carving 20 minutes per day out of the literacy block to work with a small group of struggling readers while the other students are working independently should be a top priority and will provide the extra bit of instruction that can make a world of difference for these students.

Structuring Reading Groups

Response to Intervention (RTI) research tells us that about 85% of our students should respond to the regular curriculum and be able to cope with grade-level texts and tasks. Another 3% to 5% are likely to have issues that could require long-term, if not permanent, external support from special education. It is the remaining 10% to 12% of students, therefore, who are most likely to benefit from that "extra scoop" of classroom instruction. Even in a class of 30 students, there shouldn't be more than about six students who require special attention. (If a much higher percentage of students struggle with the regular classroom program, then perhaps the program needs to be reconsidered.)

There are many ways to group students for instruction (see the Grouping Structures chart below). Some groupings are interest-based; literature circle groups, for example, are formed around students engaged in reading and discussing the same book. Other groupings are random; we might ask students to turn and talk to the person beside them or to conduct a peer conference with a partner of their choice. For small-group reading instruction, however, reading groups are generally organized by common need—usually reading level or strategy. Some teachers, painfully recalling the "three reading groups" from days of yore, are uncomfortable with what they perceive as "ability" grouping. Let's not forget that these students' self-esteem has already taken a beating from spending three or more school years as struggling readers. Twenty minutes a day in a group where the teaching, texts, and tasks are designed to foster success and growth certainly can't do any more damage to their self-image. Of course, every struggling reader is different, and the only thing this group of six might have in common is an inability to cope with grade-level texts. Ideally, we might form two groups of three or a group of four and a group of two around common needs; realistically, we might just have to deal with a somewhat divergent group. However, within a group of six, it's much easier to provide differentiated instruction and to monitor progress than within a class of thirty.

Grouping Structures in the Reading Block

	Guided Reading (Instructional)	Literature Circles/ Discussion Groups	Reading Workshop
Grouping	Groups of 4–8, based on reading levels and/or strategy needs	Groups of 4–8, based on choice and interest in reading a particular text	Individual
Reading Materials	• Texts are matched to instructional level of students, chosen by the teacher • Short texts and excerpts	• Texts represent a range of reading levels and topics, though they may have a common theme or genre	• Self-selected, often with teacher guidance • Full-length novels and other texts
		• Students select from a range offered by the teacher • Generally novels, but can include full-length nonfiction texts	

	Guided Reading (Instructional)	*Literature Circles/ Discussion Groups*	*Reading Workshop*
Instructional Focus	Focus on the reader rather than the text; skill and strategy work based on assessed needs of the group of students	Focus on the text: content, literary elements, text structure, personal response	Focus on both the reader (strategies) and the text (content); it tends to be more incidental than systematic.
Leadership	Teacher-led	Student-led	Student self-directed, with teacher conferences
Advantages	Provides instructional scaffolding and support at the point of need	Creates opportunity for authentic response to reading and discussion	Builds independence and individual instruction
Disadvantages	"Ability" grouping might not expose students to more-complex literature or literary concepts	Does not offer specific strategic reading support	Contact with teacher is brief and less frequent; fewer opportunities to address strategy needs

It's important to take care that students are not defined or labeled by their group; the arrangement is just one of many structures for teaching and learning in the classroom. Students should spend no more than 20 minutes each day in a needs-based reading group, and should have opportunities to work in many other groups and partnerships throughout the rest of the day. That's why it's important to keep groupings flexible and change them on a regular basis. At least once a month, take time to conduct an oral reading inventory to reconsider the groupings and instructional plans.

What Does Small-Group Instruction Look Like?

Small-group reading instruction means different things to different people. In some cases, the term *guided reading* connotes a very specific structure for instruction; however, I like to think of guided reading as a small-group structure that includes whatever types of instruction, support, and scaffolded practice the students need in order to become better readers. This usually means minimizing teaching time and maximizing students' reading time. In a small-group guided reading session, we want students to achieve two main things: to build the competencies of good readers and to understand and appreciate text.

Here are some guidelines for small-group reading instruction:

1. Keep the lessons short and focused

A 20-minute time frame is adequate to address one or two specific learning goals, dig into an appropriate text, and keep the students engaged. After all, we're going to go back and read that text again. If we want to make the most of those 20 minutes, we need to make sure that our lessons are carefully planned and focused on a specific goal or concept, to have all resources at hand, and to set a timer! If the timer goes before the lesson plan is accomplished, leave the rest of the lesson for another day.

2. Choose short texts that are engaging and accessible

In Chapter 1, we addressed choosing texts that are just a little bit challenging for the students, texts that have them *standing on their tiptoes* as readers, for small-group instruction. Texts should be short enough to be read in one sitting and to be revisited over subsequent sessions. Entire novels are generally not appropriate for small-group guided reading. For one thing, the kind of close reading and rereading of the text done in small-group instruction would make a novel study tedious and tiring. Moreover, literary novels usually have peaks and valleys in their level of difficulty, with some chapters too difficult for your students and others too easy. However, carefully chosen excerpts or individual chapters of novels can be excellent texts for small-group reading, and sometimes the lesson will provide enough support for the students to read other sections on their own.

3. Revisit the same text two or three times

The research on repeated reading suggests that, if we want students to think and comprehend deeply, a text has to be read more than once (Thierren, 2004). For a challenging text, the first reading simply enables the reader to make sense of the print and get the gist of the passage. Subsequent readings build comprehension and fluency; they enable us to dive more deeply into the content of the text, to think more critically, and to appreciate the author's craft. I like to have students read each passage at least three times, which means spending at least two or three sessions—and sometimes more—on the same piece of text.

4. Introduce texts carefully

Text introductions have recently received some bad press in the literacy world (Pearson, 2013). Certainly, spending more time preparing to read a text than actually reading it is ineffective practice, but some form of text introduction is particularly important for struggling readers. These students need guidance in applying appropriate background knowledge to making meaning, in setting purposes for reading and adjusting their reading to those purposes. Previewing a text before reading not only supports this practice, but is also one of the habits of highly effective readers.

Three *Ps* of Prereading
- Preview the Text
- Activate *Prior* Knowledge
- Set a *Purpose* for Reading

The text introduction should be brief and intentional, and it should support essential reading habits. I use a quick, three-part introduction: preview the text, activate prior knowledge, and set a purpose for reading. Setting a purpose helps us take a stance as readers and guides us in knowing how to approach the reading; for example, we will approach the text quite differently if we know it's intended to make us laugh than if we know it's intended to teach a complex concept. The length of the text introduction will vary according to the challenges of the text and the amount of background knowledge students will need, but I try to keep it as brief as possible. Planning my text introduction ahead of time helps me make the most of the brief 20-minute session.

5. Have students read individually and silently

During small-group instruction, students should have their own copies of the text and be reading to themselves, except when instructed to read for the teacher. As my students read silently, I tap the book of one student at a time, indicating that the student should read aloud in a soft voice for my ears only. I only need to listen for 15 or 20 seconds to know how a student is coping with the text before moving on to the next student.

No reader—especially a struggling reader—should be asked to read publicly without having an opportunity to rehearse first. On subsequent rereadings, I will ask students to read sections aloud, but always with a purpose for both the reader and the listeners. Because students are reading silently, we read only short chunks of text before stopping to discuss both the content of the text and the reading process.

6. Provide lots of opportunities for literate talk about text

Literate talk refers to discussion that requires students to analyze characters, interpret events, draw inferences, make comparisons and contrasts, read critically, and generally think more deeply about text. During a 20-minute small-group reading lesson, there isn't much time for writing, but there should be lots of time for discussion that helps students to think more deeply and critically about what they've read and to be more metacognitive about the processes they have used as readers.

As part of my lesson planning, I predetermine "pause points" in the reading, and prepare questions and prompts that will guide students to interpret the text and extend their thinking to higher levels.

7. Plan a follow-up task

Even the most finely executed lesson will be wasted if the students never apply what they've learned to reading on their own. *Must-do* tasks generally entail more reading and/or writing to practice a strategy, reinforce a new concept, or extend the experience with the text. Of course, must-do tasks are always linked to the specific learning goals of the lesson, but might include routines like the following:

- Read another section of text and track thinking with sticky notes
- Take turns reading aloud with a partner to build fluency
- Play a game that involves vocabulary development or a word-solving strategy, such as building words with prefixes and suffixes.
- Complete a graphic organizer or other written response

The Guided Reading Lesson Planner

Making the most of limited time with a small group requires careful planning and organization.

> **Three-Day Lesson Cycle**
> Day 1: Testing the Waters: Introduce the text and have students read it independently to get the gist of it.
> Day 2: Diving Deeper: Do a closer reading of the text to focus on interpreting content, building metacognition, and reading critically.
> Day 3: Dipping Back In: Skim, scan, or closely reread the text to focus on vocabulary, word-solving, fluency, and writer's craft.

The planner shown here uses a three-day lesson cycle. Reading on the first day is like dipping a toe in a pool to get the temperature; i.e., it is generally dedicated to introducing the text and "first-draft" reading. In texts that stretch a reader, the first reading often enables us just to navigate the print and get a sense of what it's all about. If we want to understand more thoroughly, we usually need to read it again. Therefore, on the second day, we dive more deeply into the text to talk about what the author has said and how he/she has said it. We might reread with a focus on one or more comprehension strategies. Finally, on a third reading, we dip back into certain sections of the text to practice word-solving strategies, to reread for fluency, to focus on text features, or to analyze literary elements.

The Small-Group Lesson Planner on page 24 is a lesson planning template that you can use to set goals for instruction, prepare a text introduction, and plan a three-day cycle of instruction, guided reading, and must-do practice.

Sample Small-Group Lesson Cycle

The text used for the sample lesson cycle on page 23 is Chapter 1 from *Ghost House* by Paul Kropp; see Appendix A, pages 142–143 for excerpted pages. The reading level of this chapter (and the entire book) is mid-Grade 3.

Sample Lesson Plan

Learning Focus	Text
Comprehension: Drawing inferences about characters **Word/Language Study:** Apostrophes for possessives and contractions	*Ghost House*, Chapter 1

Preview: *This is a book about three boys who dare each other to spend the night in an old house that they think is haunted.*

Prior Knowledge: *TTYN (Talk to your Neighbor) about what story elements you might expect to find in a book about a haunted house.*

Purpose: *We know that there are three ways we learn about characters when we read: from what the author says directly about them, from what they say and do, and from what others say to and about them. In this chapter, we learn about the four main characters: Tyler, Zach, AJ, Hammy. As you read, think about each of the characters. At the end, we're going to talk about what we know about each character—and how we learned about them.*

Day 1	Must-Do
- Book introduction - Read pages 3–4 aloud while students follow. Talk about what has been learned about the characters so far and how this information is conveyed. (Zach: little brother; Hammy: good skateboarder; Tyler: big brother, smart mouth, not afraid; AJ: real name Alexander; All four characters: like to laugh, friends, hang out together.) Create a character chart, sorted as *In the Book* (literal) and *In My Head* (inferential). Require students to find evidence in the text. - Put a stop sign at the end of page 7 and have students read silently. (Teacher taps on a student's book as a signal for that student to raise his/her voice, and listens to each student in turn for a few seconds.) - Stop and talk: *What can we add to the character chart?*	- Finish reading the chapter. - Create your own character chart from paper folded in half with columns labeled *In the Book/In My Head*. Jot 2–3 things learned about each of the three main characters.
Day 2	**Must-Do**
- Revisit must-do task. Be sure students understand the difference between a trait (good skateboarder) and evidence from the text ("Hammy did a 180 ollie that looked pretty slick."). Add new ideas to the group character chart. - Review the characteristics of good oral reading: volume, expression, phrasing, pacing. Have students reread the chapter aloud in pairs, taking turns reading half-pages; listen in on individual students and take anecdotal notes. - Discuss: What do you think of the dare? Are the stakes equal? Which characters do you predict will stay in the house? Why do you think so?	Create a Venn diagram to compare the characters of Tyler and Hammy.
Day 3	**Must-Do**
- Invite students to read their must-do responses aloud. - Language/Word study: apostrophes. Have students scan the text for examples of words with apostrophes and use highlighting tape to mark them. Create a chart labeled *Possessives* and *Contractions* to sort the words. - Discussion: *How do you think the boys should prepare for the night in the haunted house? What should they do to let someone know where they are in case something happens to them?*	Extended Response: As Tyler, write a note to your mom, explaining what you are doing and why you feel you have to do it. Your response should have three parts: 1) where you are going to be overnight 2) why you decided to stay overnight in the haunted house 3) why she shouldn't be angry with you

Small-Group Lesson Planner

Learning Focus	Text

Preview:

Prior Knowledge:

Purpose:

Day 1	Must-Do

Day 2	Must-Do

Day 3	Must-Do

© 2014 *Struggling Readers* by Lori Jamison Rog. Pembroke Publishers. ISBN 978-1-55138-292-0

3

Struggling Readers Need to Read a Lot More

According to a wise philosopher named Dr. Seuss, "the more you read, the more you know; the more you know, the more places you'll go." We may never convince some of our students that reading is fun or even satisfying, but no one can deny that reading makes a person smarter. The research is clear. The more kids read, the better readers they will be. Or is it the better readers kids are, the more they will read? No one's quite sure which is the cause and which the effect. But the bottom line is that there is a significant correlation between quantity of reading and proficiency of reading. Individuals who read a lot develop more vocabulary and background knowledge; they also experience a range of syntactic structures and literary elements that enable them to understand and appreciate increasingly complex text. In a series of studies, Anne Cunningham and Keith Stanovich (1998) found that extensive reading was linked to superior performance on measures of general knowledge, vocabulary, spelling, verbal fluency, and reading comprehension—even among students with lower general ability.

The chart below summarizes some of the data from Richard Anderson and his colleagues' classic study. Kids scoring at the 90th percentile on standardized tests read, on average, 40 minutes a day, whereas kids scoring at the 10th percentile did not read at all outside of school (Anderson, Wilson & Fielding 1984). Particularly compelling is the connection between reading and exposure to vocabulary. Approximately 5 to 10% of new words encountered in reading are retained (Stahl, 1999) and it's generally accepted that every new word learned leads to an increase of at least three more words in the reader's vocabulary (Schumm, Moody & Vaughn, 2000).

Relationship Between Independent Reading and Reading Test Scores, Fifth Grade

Achievement Percentile on Standardized Reading Tests	Average Minutes of Reading per Day	Words Read in a Year	Words Read in a Year: Additional 10 Minutes Reading a Day	Percent Increase in Number of Words Read
90th	21.1	1,823,000	2,686,981	47%
50th	4.6	282,000	895,403	217%
20th	<1	21,000	321,000	1428%

Just do the math! With an increase of only 10 minutes per day of school reading time, our most needy readers will go from reading 20,000 words to more than 300,000 words—an increase of almost 1500%! Even our "average" (50th percentile) kids will increase the number of words they are exposed to by more than

200%. The solution seems simple: we need to increase the amount of time spent on independent reading in school.

Well, perhaps it's not as simple as it sounds. In 2000, the National Reading Panel in the U.S. rocked the reading world with its finding of inadequate research to support the effectiveness of Sustained Silent Reading (SSR) in improving reading proficiency. Many researchers quickly discounted the report as flawed by the panel's limits on the parameters of scientific research, rejecting descriptive and qualitative research. Meanwhile, just as many school administrators jerked their knees and banned silent reading time, sending students back to the basals.

Even those of us who would never abandon our SSR programs must agree that some independent reading routines are more effective than others. For one thing, kids have to be interested in what they are reading. For another thing, readers need texts that are at an appropriate level of difficulty—neither too difficult nor too easy.

Scaffolded Silent Reading

How can we make our Independent Reading programs as effective as possible? Ray Reutzel and his colleagues (2008) have identified several conditions of effective *scaffolded silent reading* practices, including the following:

1. Student Self-Selection of Reading Material—With Support

Choice is an essential element of effective independent reading programs. However, students don't always know how to find the best books for themselves. That's why teachers need to know both their students and their books. Guiding individual students to the right book can make all the difference to them as readers. With help, students will learn to choose books that interest them and that are just right in terms of difficulty. There's no satisfaction in reading books that are too hard; by the same token, most sixth-grade readers aren't going to find much of interest in a book designed for eight-year-olds. On the other hand, we know that even a reluctant reader will work through a text if he/she is really motivated to read it. And even capable readers often like to choose easier texts for independent reading. There's a place for teacher-selected challenging texts in the instructional block, but independent reading is for easy reading practice. We need to empower students and honor their choices, while ever nudging them to extend their reach in content, genre, and degree of difficulty.

Teacher book talks are a great way to introduce books that students might not discover on their own. Have you noticed that, whenever we offer kids a choice of books, they always gravitate toward the ones that have been recommended by the teacher or other students? It doesn't take much time to scan a book and offer a quick sales pitch. When students have books they can and want to read, they are more likely to be engaged, interested, and motivated to read more. Take a few minutes to promote a couple of books each day, and try to allow time before or after independent reading for students to talk to others about what they're reading.

Where to get book recommendations
- **From friends and classmates**
- **From parents, teachers, or librarians**
- **Reading the back-cover blurb**
- **Finding another book by the same author**
- **Websites like Shelfari (www. shelfari.com) or Goodreads (www.goodreads.com)**

Elements of a Pithy Promo

1. Introduce the title and author and show the cover art.
2. Read aloud the back cover (or inside flyleaf) blurb.
3. Make a personal observation: e.g., "This book is quite scary" or "This ending is going to surprise you" or "This is a book for readers who like..."

2. Student Accountability

I've always felt that independent reading time should be about enjoying reading and not having to be accountable for what's been read. On the other hand, too many students—especially struggling readers—are neither enjoying nor even reading during this time. (Remember my student Charlie, who spent the entire reading time at the bookshelf, "choosing a book"?) If we want our Sustained Silent Reading (SSR) program to be as effective as it can be, we need to ensure that students are actually reading. On the other hand, it's important that accountability tasks don't distract from the reading itself. Particularly with struggling readers, we need to be cautious about loading too many written assignments onto reading, as they simply make a difficult task even more unpleasant. Completing book reports—whether cereal box dioramas or illustrated storyboards—does little to teach anyone to be a better reader, and certainly has never encouraged a reluctant reader to pick up a book.

My compromise is to have students complete a simple reading log. Some teachers advocate reading websites like Shelfari or Goodreads, which invite readers to record and review the books they've read. I prefer to use the individual Independent Reading Log on page 35, in which students briefly note the genre, difficulty, and appeal of each book, as well as the title, author, and length of the books they read. It's useful for students to keep track of their own reading, and especially handy for struggling readers to have a record of their accomplishments. As well, using the Reading Log helps me informally monitor what my students are reading, what they're finishing, and what they're enjoying.

3. Interactions of Teachers and Students around Texts

Social interaction about reading can motivate wide reading and expand experiences with text; we see this in the popularity of book clubs. One of the best ways for students to account for what they've read is to have them talk about their reading with other students. But interactions between teachers and students are even more important, according to Reutzel and his colleagues. We used to think that the teacher's role during silent reading time was to model reading him/herself. While personal reading provided a pretty peaceful way for us to spend 20 minutes of class time, it really didn't contribute much to our students' reading development. In truth, the best way we can spend our time is by circulating among students to talk about their reading, to listen to them read, and to suggest other reading. As we confer with students as they read, we can ask questions:

- What's your reading about?
- Are you enjoying this book? What do you like or dislike about it?
- What kinds of reading do you usually prefer?
- Would you please read this page/paragraph to me?
- Do you think you might enjoy...?

As a quick assessment of both fluency and comprehension, invite each student to prepare a one-minute oral reading from their books.

In a 20-minute SSR period, it should be possible to meet with three or four students and record brief anecdotal notes on your conversations, thereby meeting with every student every few weeks. This is also a good time to conduct individual oral reading assessments (see page 11).

You might establish a routine of starting (or ending) each SSR period with a teacher or student book talk. Schedule two or three students per day to share their reading, or break students into groups to share in pairs or small groups.

Launching the Independent Reading Program

With luck, your students are accustomed to reading independently and you'll be able to get your SSR program up and running the first week of school. But chances are, you'll have a few—or several—students who don't have the independence and self-regulation to read for 20 minutes right off the bat. Here are some tips for getting started with an effective SSR program.

1. Build SSR into your timetable for at least 20 minutes every day

Consider when independent reading will be most effective. At the beginning of the day, will it be interrupted by late arrivals or daily routines? At the end of the day, will it be neglected in the preparations for dismissal? It might be necessary to start with shorter time frames and gradually have students build stamina for reading, especially with younger students and struggling readers. From the first day, keep a timer on hand and record how long the whole class is able to read without interruption. (Some teachers like to keep a graph of reading stamina times visible in the classroom.) Gradually, all your students should be able to read independently for 20 minutes or more.

2. Establish norms and routines to be practiced by and expected of all students

Reading time is for reading. Students don't exchange books, do homework, or chat during this time. All students need to take responsibility for having their reading materials on hand for reading time. If they have nothing else to read, they might have to resort to their science text book, an old basal reader from a previous grade, or a book provided by the teacher. They'll soon learn that they'd rather make the choice themselves. Collaborate with the students to create a set of Readers' Rights and Responsibilities and enforce these consistently as the norms for your classroom's independent reading program.

Sample Readers' Rights and Responsibilities

We have the right to	We have the responsibility to
• *Choose the books we want to read* • *Not be disturbed by others when we're reading* • *Reread a book or part of a book that we enjoyed* • *Abandon a book that is not interesting* • *Read where we want in the classroom, as long as it's not disturbing others*	• *Test drive a book before abandoning it* • *Keep a log of what we read* • *Avoid disturbing others* • *Have our books on hand for daily reading time* • *Share what we're reading and recommend good books to others*

3. Help students build independent learning habits

The whole point of independent reading time is independence. There are many other times during the day when the teacher will choose what, when, and how students will read and how they will respond to their reading. At this time, we want students to learn to select their own books, to document their own reading, and to solve their own problems.

You might want to teach techniques for choosing books; for example how to preview a book:

- Start by reading the information (called a "blurb") on the back cover or flyleaf.
- Then open the book at random and read a page. Does it seem easy or hard? Are there too many difficult words on the page? Try the High-Five trick to see how hard the book might be for you.
- Try another page. Does it seem interesting to you? Is it interesting enough that you're willing to slog through some hard parts?

> **High-Five**
>
> Here's a quick strategy to judge whether a book is too hard for you. Open the book to any page. As you read the page, give the book a high-five by holding up your hand with the fingers out. Each time your come to a word you don't know or an idea that you don't understand, put one finger down. If you have a fist by the end of the page or before, the book is probably not right for you. Try again with a few more pages, to be sure.

4. Make sure that students have books that are engaging and accessible

You will need to establish your own routines for school library visits and for supplementing reading with materials from classroom and home libraries. Having a book collection in the classroom ensures that students will have access to books at any time. It has been suggested that a classroom library should contain 20 books per student; that's practically 600 books for an average intermediate classroom. But the books do not all need to be on display at any time; in fact, the collection should be recycled on a regular basis. Try to keep samples of a range of genres and reading levels, including nontraditional texts such as brochures and manuals. Magazines, manuals, and newspapers also make popular reading choices.

What to Read

Novels and Chapter Books

Novels and chapter books have long been the preferred genres for school reading, and with good reason. In a world of sound bites and 140-character messages, SSR time provides the ideal opportunity to build the stamina needed to read a lengthy text.

One of the challenges for struggling readers in reading trade books (i.e., books for the general public, sold by booksellers) is that the reading difficulty is likely to rise and fall several times throughout the book. These books were written for their thought-provoking content and literary craft, not to support a reader who struggles. Some publishers will print a grade level on the back of a book (the kiss of death in the eyes of a struggling reader); however, this usually means that the publisher has taken an average of all the words and sentences in an entire book. Katherine Patterson's *Bridge to Terabithia,* for example, is frequently read

Remember that independent reading time is for building confidence as well as competence in reading; in other words, easy reading. Don't be too concerned if *Diary of a Wimpy Kid* and *The Hunger Games* fly off the shelves, while *The Complete Works of Shakespeare* collects dust.

in Grade 5 classrooms. The Flesch-Kincaid grade level readability is 4.4, which sounds pretty manageable. But in truth, this average likely means that there are some sections with readability as low as Grade 2 and that some might be as high as Grade 8. If we decide that every fifth-grader in our class needs to experience *Bridge to Terabithia,* then we should use it as a read-aloud rather than have them read it themselves.

Hi-Lo Books

High-interest/low-vocabulary, or hi-lo, books are written especially for struggling readers. At their best, they contain interesting stories or information, written in a readable style with vocabulary controls and other text features to support readers. Of course, as with any other product, some are better than others. There are many books that profess to be hi-lo that are neither interesting to kids nor easy to read.

When looking for high-interest/low-vocabulary reading materials for struggling readers, the two most important considerations are content and appearance. Both novels and nonfiction should be about themes of interest to students of the appropriate age. Just because a twelve-year-old reads at Grade 2 level doesn't mean that he/she wants to read the things that seven-year-olds read. And we want to find books that don't look different from the books that other students are reading. In terms of book length, the Goldilocks Principle applies: the book has to be long enough to look like a "regular" novel or chapter book, but not so long as to intimidate striving readers. Publishers use different tricks for padding out an otherwise short novel: occasional illustrations, starting each chapter halfway down the page, slightly enlarged spaces between lines. However, be careful to avoid oversized print and unusual fonts: large print might appeal to those of us needing reading glasses, but it might as well flash "*SPECIAL*" in neon lights in the eyes of adolescents. Some other considerations in choosing quality hi-lo books include

- consistent level of difficulty throughout the book
- more action than description
- age-appropriate illustrations that provide visual support for understanding the text
- authentic characters that are older than the readers
- a limited number of challenging words or figurative language, with contextual support for difficult words
- few literary devices, such as flashback, foreshadowing, or allusion

Informational Texts

Novels are not the only source of reading materials for students. Many of our students, especially boys, are more engaged by informational reading, as long as it matches their interests and abilities. Fortunately, there is a wealth of nonfiction available to our students on every topic imaginable, from witchcraft to warfare, from extreme sports to tsunamis. Why does nonfiction appeal to so many of our struggling readers? Look at the *Guinness Book of World Records* (a guaranteed favorite with boys) and you'll notice the following:

- Information is presented in chunks; that is, you don't have to hold an entire book full of details in your head in order to understand the plot. In fact, you don't even need to read the entire book. You can read only the sections that interest you.

- There are plenty of visual supports—illustrations, headings, bold or colored print—which also means there is more white space and less text density on the page.
- There are many text-structure and vocabulary supports, such as topic sentences, context clues, and even definitions and pronunciation keys.
- It contains "cool stuff."

Chapters 8 and 9 offer many ideas for supporting strategic reading of informational and functional texts.

In spite of the additional supports in informational texts, nonfiction can be more difficult than fiction for readers at all ages and stages. For one thing, authors assume that the reader is bringing certain background knowledge on the topic to the reading. There is often technical vocabulary related to the topic that might or might not be defined in the text. And nonfiction text structures frequently require nonlinear reading; a traditional top-to-bottom, left-to-right progression might leave out key information or find it in the wrong order. Teaching students the unique strategies necessary for reading nonfiction can open the door to many more reading possibilities.

Functional Texts

Functional texts are the texts that we need to read in order to function in a literate world: street signs, directions, maps, labels, websites, and brochures, to name just a few. Reading the directions to complete a model (or, for teens, a driving manual to obtain a driver's license) provides the motivation many readers need to use reading for a purpose. Including functional texts in our classroom libraries sends students the message that reading isn't just something we do in school; it's an important thing we do in life.

E-Books

In 2000, in a massive meta-analysis of the research on reading instruction, the National Reading Panel reported that computer technology had potential for supporting reading instruction. Today, the best we can say is that technology continues to have potential. In fact, a major study undertaken by the U.S. Department of Education in 2007 found that there was no significant difference in reading achievement between those students who used educational software and those who did not (Trotter, 2007).

The greatest potential for digital reading support may very well come in the form of e-readers. E-books appear to have definite bonuses for struggling readers: minimal print on the page, ability to control the appearance of the page, the feeling of accomplishment with each page turn, and sometimes even links to word definitions and pronunciations. Not to mention the fact that every book looks the same on an e-reader, so no one can tell that one student is reading an easy novel while another is reading a very difficult one.

But the challenges are also significant. At this relatively early stage of e-book development, many publishers seem to be more careless about errors and formatting than with print books. For example, in a biography of Catherine the Great I read recently, the publisher did not use font or spacing techniques to distinguish between the narrative and the actual excerpts from Catherine's diary, as would have been done in a print book. (This was challenging enough for me as an effective reader; it would be disastrous for a struggling reader.) As well, many teachers are unfamiliar with how to use the e-book format for guiding students through texts, not to mention being challenged by managing the behavior of students who profess to be reading while actually playing video games or surfing the Internet. It will take significant effort on the parts of both teachers and publishers for e-books to reach their potential as instructional tools.

Audio Books

Audio books expose readers to texts and genres that they are unable to read on their own. They help students build vocabulary and background knowledge, enhancing comprehension. Although there are many benefits of audio books, the reality is that the students are listening to the text, not reading it.

What about giving kids a copy of the book to follow along with the reading they hear? Some publishers call this practice "shared reading." In truth, the only sharing that's going on is when the students hear a bell and all turn the page at the same time. Our struggling readers simply don't read quickly enough to follow along with a fluent adult reader. Some programmed learning materials claim to be able to slow down the reading to enable the struggling reader to keep up. But slowing down the reading that much eliminates the best parts of a professional read-aloud—fluency, pacing, and expression. Having struggling readers toil to match the marks on the page with the wonderfully expressive reading they're hearing detracts from both processes. We need to carefully consider whether this is the best way to spend independent reading time.

Graphic Novels

Getting kids to read comics has never been a hard sell, and graphic novels have come a long way from the comic books of old. The term *comic book* refers to any format that uses a combination of sequential art, minimal narration, and frames to tell a story. By that definition, graphic novels are actually comic books, though they tend to be longer, be bound in covers like other books, and contain a complete story rather than part of a serial.

Today's readers live in a visual world: TV, websites, on-demand movies, and video games. Graphic novels take advantage of that experience with visually appealing, high-action themes. While traditional graphic novels were often, well, *graphic,* today's graphic novels have gone beyond scantily dressed women and violent or sexual overtones. The genre today contains content for all ages and stages of reading and ranges from the popular fantasy, superhero, and ghost stories (90% of all graphic novels) to biographies, historical stories, and news reports. A fairly recent innovation in the world of literature, the graphic novel has exploded in popularity over the past decade, especially among adolescent males (Botzakis, 2009). Increasing numbers of graphic novels are being written—and well-written—specifically for adolescent and teen readers. Graphic novels often appeal to struggling readers because the texts may be (but are not always) shorter; they are also a quicker read than a traditional text-based novel because of the illustrative supports. Unfortunately, research on the extent to which graphic novels are actually helping kids become better readers is scant, but any material that gets kids reading has got to be worthy of consideration.

One concern with graphic novels for struggling readers is that they are not necessarily easy reading. The text, while minimal, is not controlled for vocabulary or sentence structure. The plots are often complex and require a great deal of inference to bridge the gap between picture and text or from one scene to another. Advocates of graphic novels argue that the illustrations provide adequate support for challenging vocabulary or complex plot lines; I worry that it's too easy to avoid the words entirely (or at least the difficult ones) and read only the pictures to get the gist of the storyline. In fact, it has been suggested that comic book readers can usually understand up to 70% of a story from the pictures alone (Gorman 2003).

Just because a book looks like a comic doesn't mean that it will be easy to read. Consider this excerpt from *The Anne Frank House Authorized Graphic Biography*: "Miles upon miles of trenches confronted each other across a wasted no-man's land, a stalemate that weapons such as poison gas and machine guns did not alter" (p. 9). The grammatical constructs and choice of words could stymie even a competent reader!

That said, there is plenty of evidence, both empirical and anecdotal, that graphic novels have motivated many reluctant readers to read more. And we know from research on reading volume that there is a definite connection between more reading and better reading. As teachers, we still need to pay careful attention to helping students find graphic novels that are just right in terms of both difficulty and interest. We also need to teach students the unique strategies for reading graphic novels. Some teaching points include

- Directionality: From panel to panel and within panels, graphic novels are read from top left to bottom right, taking in all the information in each panel: caption boxes, speech balloons, thought clouds, and pictures.
- Reading pictures: The pictures essentially tell the story in a graphic novel. Teach students to look carefully at the pictures for clues about characters' thoughts and feelings, changing actions, events and scenes, and clues to what is going to happen next.
- Connecting pictures and print: Print is intended to provide information that the pictures can't (and vice versa). Take time to talk about what information is provided only in the picture and what information is only in the text. Draw attention to how the two interact to tell the story.
- Artistic style: Comic book art has unique characteristics and techniques, such as *crosshatching* (short lines to create a shadow), *speed lines* (short parallel lines to indicate fast movement), and *silhouette* (outline of a person or object, usually shaded in black). The graphic organizer on page 36 can be used to analyze features of a particular graphic novel.
- Symbols: Cartoon drawing is full of graphic devices that add emotions, sounds, and movements to the page. Have students keep a log of these symbols as they are encountered; you might choose to teach some of the silly names developed by comic strip creator Mort Walker (the creator of the Beetle Bailey and Hi & Lois comics); see box on page 34. The graphic organizer on page 36 can be used to record examples that students find.

> **Mort Walker's Names for Comic Strip Symbols**
> Briffits: Clouds of dust that trail behind fast-moving characters
> Hites: Horizontal lines that trail behind fast-moving characters to indicate motion
> Dites: Diagonal lines placed across glass surfaces to indicate sheen
> Grawlixes: Symbols that indicate swearing or angry talk
> Plewds: Drops of sweat from a character's head to indicate nervousness, stress, or hard work
> Solrads: Lines proceeding from a light source
> Emanata: Lines that surround a character's head to indicate surprise or shock
> Agitrons: Long wiggly lines around something that is shaking or vibrating

Books for Boys

A discussion of struggling readers would be incomplete without some mention of the unique challenges of finding books for boys. The reality is that the majority of our struggling readers are boys, and we need to make extra effort to find books that our boys can and will want to read. It goes without saying that every boy is different, but there are some generalities we can pay attention to when helping boys find books to read. Paul Kropp, author of more than 50 books for young adult readers, suggests that we *BEAR* these things in mind when selecting fiction for boys:

- **B**oys or men as main characters
- **E**pisodic as opposed to a rising plot line
- **A**ction-oriented plots
- **R**ebellious characters

To read an interview with author Paul Kropp on engaging boys in reading, go to http://www.hip-books.com/teachers/the_boy_problem_in_reading/

Informational texts and graphic novels seem to have particular appeal for boys, who tend to be oriented more toward visual/spatial learning than girls (Ontario Ministry of Education, 2008). Graphic novels contain many features that appeal to boy readers—fantastic content (as in fantasy and superheroes), action-packed storylines, visual appeal, and a connection to popular culture.

One of the reasons so many of our boys lose interest in reading is that school reading tends to discourage the very kinds of reading boys are willing to do. Author Jon Scieszka has created a website called Guys Read (www.guysread.com) that encourages boys to read and to recommend books for other boys. Among the categories of endorsed titles are books about space, with or without aliens; books on war; robots or how to build stuff; and books with at least one explosion. Taking the extra time to find a particular book for a particular boy could very well result in the match made in heaven that hooks him as a reader for life.

Independent Reading Log

Date	Title and Author	Pages	Did you finish it?	Did you like it?	Had you read it before?	Easy, Medium, or Hard	Genre

© 2014 *Struggling Readers* by Lori Jamison Rog. Pembroke Publishers. ISBN 978-1-55138-292-0

Analyzing a Graphic Novel

Which of these cartooning techniques can you find?

	What the artist did	**What it means**
Time of day, month, or year		
Sounds		
Character emotions		
Movement		
Talking or speech		

© 2014 *Struggling Readers* by Lori Jamison Rog. Pembroke Publishers. ISBN 978-1-55138-292-0

4

Struggling Readers Need to Be Taught What Good Readers Do

Here's a little reading test:

Up sleep peaches after happy green from.

Got it? The vocabulary is simple, your decoding is automatic, and no doubt you can put the words together quite fluently. So what's the problem? Comprehension, that's what! Welcome to the world of the struggling reader. All too often, struggling readers can decode and pronounce the words, but something breaks down between the individual words and the overall comprehension. Comprehension is more than just barking out words; it's about making sense of text. That's the thing about reading; it's all about comprehension.

There was a time when some educators believed that decoding skills and print concepts could be taught, but that comprehension simply happened as long as the reader could connect the marks on the page to sounds and words. They thought, in other words, that comprehension was *caught* rather than *taught*. It's true that comprehension just seems to happen when the reading is easy. But when the text contains challenging vocabulary or complex concepts, or when the reader doesn't have the requisite background knowledge, then comprehension breaks down. That's why comprehension must be taught.

One of the challenges of reading instruction is that reading is an invisible, in-the-head process. You can't see what readers are doing when they read and there's no product to use as a model or a demonstration of learning. That's why we've historically tended to "teach" reading by simply asking questions about a text that has been read. The problem with this technique is that it doesn't help students learn how to read better. Today we know that if we want our students to become better readers, we need to teach them what good readers do.

Teaching Comprehension Strategies

Thanks to the work of David Pearson, Nell Duke, and others, we now know that there are a handful of specific, teachable strategies that readers use to make sense of text. In fact, there is evidence that the deliberate and purposeful use of even one of these comprehension strategies can have an impact on a student's overall comprehension (Duke & Pearson, 2002). Many readers develop these strategies easily; for struggling readers, the strategies must be explicitly taught, reinforced, practiced, and taught again.

Comprehension strategies include
- Setting purposes for reading
- Previewing and predicting
- Making connections to prior knowledge
- Monitoring, clarifying, and repairing
- Visualizing and creating visual representations
- Asking and answering questions
- Drawing inferences and making judgments
- Summarizing and synthesizing
- Using text structures

In a two-year study, Grade 5 students who were taught to focus on the content of text actually had a better understanding of the comprehension strategies used to access it than students who were taught to focus mainly on the strategies themselves (McKeown, Beck & Blake, 2009).

Many teachers today follow comprehension curricula suggested by Ellin Keene and Susan Zimmerman (2007) or Stephanie Harvey and Anne Goudvis (2007), which focus on one strategy at a time. Other approaches, such as the Common Core State Standards initiative, focus more on the content and structure of the texts themselves than on the reading process. I believe it's quite possible—and quite effective—to balance both process and content. For example, as we guide discussion of a specific text, we use academic vocabulary—telling students to "infer," "predict," "visualize," or "provide evidence"—that helps readers become metacognitive about the processes they use as they construct meaning from the text.

If we want our students to become better readers, we need to teach them what good readers do, then guide them in practicing those habits of highly effective readers. This chapter will focus on three key teaching actions: modeling through think-alouds, asking effective questions, and generating literate talk about texts.

Nell Duke and David Pearson remind us that even the best comprehension instruction won't work if students don't have lots of time for sustained reading for authentic purposes. Students need to experience a range of genres, in an environment rich in high quality talk about texts and with many opportunities to express ideas through writing.

The Strategies vs Skills Debate

Strategies and *skills* are both tools for reading. The difference is that skills are actions we perform automatically—like breathing—and strategies are actions we take intentionally. "Strategies are procedural, purposeful, effortful, willful, essential, and facilitative in nature" (Alexander, Graham & Harris, 1998).

For example, when a movie runs through a reader's head while he/she reads, visualization can be seen as a skill. But when a reader pauses to take a picture in his/her mind or organize information in a pictorial way, visualization is a strategy. For beginning readers, blending sounds is a strategy they use to solve unfamiliar words; for most mature readers, letter–sound analysis occurs automatically as a skill.

Generally speaking, we're more inclined to use skills when the going is easy and strategies when the going is more difficult. For example, when driving a car, sometimes we seem to be on autopilot; it's like the car is driving itself. That's when driving is a skill. But when we hit a patch of ice, or suddenly have to maneuver around construction on the road, we'd better have a repertoire of driving strategies at our disposal to get safely to where we're going.

Thinking Aloud

According to Nell Duke and David Pearson,

> thinking aloud has been shown to improve students' comprehension both when students engage in the practice during reading and also when teachers routinely think aloud while reading to students. (Duke & Pearson, 2002: 214)

As the teacher models his/her own thinking aloud, the students gradually learn to think along until, ultimately, they are thinking alone about their own reading. Thinking aloud leads readers to be more thoughtful and strategic, to better monitor their own comprehension, and to become metacognitive about their own reading processes (Bereiter & Bird, 1985).

Think Aloud/Think Along/Think Alone

Based on work done by Roger Farr and Jenny Conner (2004), the Think Aloud/Think Along/Think Alone protocol uses a gradual release of responsibility from teacher modeling, to guided practice, to independent application.

To prepare, choose a passage of text that will be interesting to students and will lend itself to higher-level thinking. Prepare ahead by planning where you will pause and what you will say. You might decide to focus on a specific strategy, such as inferring or predicting, or you might choose to make general comments about what you are thinking as you read: what you wonder, what surprises you, or what doesn't make sense to you.

You might want to enlarge the text so the whole class can see it, or provide students with their own copies of the text should they wish—and are able—to follow along. However, we need to recognize that many students who are able to comprehend a text that is read aloud will simply not be fluent enough readers to follow along as you read.

Here are three steps to gradually release responsibility from teacher think-alouds to student think-alones:

1. Teacher Thinks Aloud
Read aloud with expression and fluency, pausing intentionally to articulate your thinking about the text and your reading processes. (See sample think-aloud on page 40.)

2. Students Think Along
After modeling your thinking for several pages, continue to read aloud and pause at predetermined points for students to turn and talk to a partner about their think-alongs about the reading. (See sample prompts on page 45.)

3. Students Think Alone
Mark a text with strategically placed pause points. Provide students with individual copies of the text for them to read on their own. It's important that texts be at an appropriate level for students; i.e., challenging enough to require readers to think, but not placing so many cognitive demands on readers that the text becomes inaccessible. Have students record their thinking alone by jotting down ideas, observations, questions, or strategies. Bring together groups of students who have read the same text to share and discuss their think-alones.

If I want students to see the text as well as hear it, I prefer using an enlarged copy for shared reading rather than providing each student with his/her own copy, so I have a little more control over what and where students are reading (and, because they are looking up, I can see their faces).

Excerpt from *Caught in the Blizzard* by Paul Kropp used with permission from High Interest Publishing.

Sample Think-Aloud

Sam raised his gun to his shoulder and looked along the sightline. There it was – the herd of caribou he'd come to hunt. In his sight was an enormous bull caribou, the largest in the herd. This bull would provide enough meat to feed his brothers and sisters for a month. Sam tugged off one mitt with his teeth and prepared to squeeze the steel-cold trigger.

"Wait," came a whisper from behind him. It was his grandfather's voice, rough from the cold.

I wonder how old Sam is. If he's with his grandfather, he's probably a kid.

Sam turned and observed the old man. The face that stared back was much like his own – round, dark, with small, sharp eyes under heavy brows. But his grandfather's face had the deep wrinkles of sixty hard years of life in the Arctic.

I know that caribou live in the far north, and from this description, I'm inferring that Sam might be Inuit.

"Go closer," his grandfather whispered hoarsely.

"They'll run off."

"If they do, they will come back," the older man replied.

Sam shook his head with doubt. His grandfather still hunted as in the old days, before guns had scopes that made the kill easy. But it was pointless to argue with him. Sam pointed the gun at the ground and paced slowly forward.

I wonder if the old ways or the new technology will be right. I'm inferring that the grandfather must be stubborn because it's pointless to argue with him.

Just as Sam had predicted, the herd fled from them. But when his grandfather stood motionless for a few minutes, the herd became curious. They turned and came back. They approached to study the two human figures outlined against the white snow and bright sky.

I think the author has phrased the last sentence in a poetic way. I can picture the dark silhouettes of Sam and his grandfather.

Asking Effective Questions

Ever since Socrates, teachers have known that asking good questions helps probe students' thinking, challenges them to extend and elaborate, and requires them to justify and support their thinking. Effective questioning is particularly important when it comes to guiding struggling readers through complex texts and helping them understand the reading processes necessary to access those texts.

In the past, many educators assumed that struggling readers couldn't cope with high-level questions. Strong readers were encouraged to think deeply, but shallow responses were accepted from immature readers; consequently, struggling readers never learned to stretch their thinking and become metacognitive about their reading processes. The scary thing is that a steady diet of one type of question teaches students to focus on that type of thinking as they read—even when we're not questioning them! Now we know that asking higher-level questions is important for all learners to stretch their thinking and extend their learning. Unfortunately, simply asking students questions that are at a higher cognitive level guarantees neither higher–cognitive-level responses nor ultimate gains in learning (Cotton, 1988). The quality of student responses can be increased by redirecting or probing further, as long as the prompts are clear and specific. The most effective probes for questioning include

- *How do you know?*
- *What evidence in the text supports your answer?*
- *Can you tell me more?*

Even simply pausing invites the student answering to expand upon his/her response.

Also important is wait time; i.e., the length of time a teacher waits between asking a question and expecting a response. Can you believe that, on average, teachers wait less than one second before providing the answer or moving on to another student? Increasing wait time even three to five seconds improves the length, depth, and quality of student responses, the level of support for their responses, and even the number of questions students generate themselves. And not only that, waiting three seconds or more after a student responds has been found to encourage elaboration and extended response (Cotton, 1988).

Question–Answer Relationships

What do effective questions look like? Almost 30 years ago, Taffy Raphael wrote about questioning in a method she called QAR, or Question–Answer Relationships. Raphael maintained that as important as the answer to a question is the relationship between the question and answer. She identified four categories of questions, maintaining that, if learners know the kind of question that is being asked, they will better know the kind of resources to draw on for the answer.

- **Right-there** questions deal with literal comprehension. There is one correct answer to a right-there question, and it is stated directly in the text. We might ask right-there questions to assess student understanding key details (*Why did the three bears go for a walk?*) but they are most effective for reinforcing concepts (*What two things are compared in the simile?*) We can also use right-there questions to help students practice scanning for details in a text.
- **Think-and-search** questions might be directly answered in the text, but generally require the reader to combine information from different places in the text. Examples of think-and-search questions that require more searching than thinking might include *What three things did Goldilocks do in the bears' house? What evidence is there that Red Riding Hood's grandmother was really the wolf?* However, some think-and-search questions require readers to synthesize information: *What is the main idea of this passage?*
- **Author-and-me** questions are inferential. They require readers to combine evidence from the text with their own background knowledge to come up with an answer that is supported by the text, but is not directly stated. When we ask inferential questions, it's important to ensure that there is supporting evidence in the text and to give students practice in finding that evidence. Inferential questions are often the most difficult for students to answer, and it's important that we teach students both to recognize author-and-me questions and to integrate textual evidence and background knowledge to answer them. Many *why* questions and prediction questions are examples of author-and-me questioning; e.g., *Why do you think the giant in Jack and the Beanstalk dislikes humans?*
- **On-my-own** questions are generally evaluative or judgmental, but might invite students to make personal connections and responses. Answers to on-my-own questions require readers to draw on their own background knowledge, experience, opinions, and feelings rather than to rely on evidence from the text. These are usually open-ended questions; there is no single correct answer. Questions such as *Do you think the character did the right thing? Why or why not?* and *What other story does this remind you of?* also generate

on-my-own answers. Because every reader is likely to come up with a different answer, these questions can generate good divergent discussions. But take care when constructing these questions to ensure that they actually require the reader to read and understand the text.

To this day, Raphael's QAR provides teachers with a structure for balancing different kinds of questions and for teaching students the processes readers draw on as they access different types of information from texts. The power of this model is that it not only helps students see a range of aspects of a given text, it also helps them develop metacognition about the way they learn as they read.

> Here's what we know about effective questioning in reading instruction:
> - Ask more high–cognitive-level questions.
> - Ask a balance of convergent (correct-answer) and divergent (open-ended) questions.
> - Wait at least 3 seconds after asking a question *and* after a student responds.
> - Use clear and specific prompts to encourage students to extend or support their responses.

Talking to Learn

There's no shortage of talk in schools. In fact, some people would argue that our classrooms are saturated with talk. The problem is, in almost every classroom, one person is doing all the talking. Interaction between teacher and students most often consists of the teacher asking a question, calling on one student to respond, then evaluating the response and moving on. In one 1999 study, fewer than 15% of all classroom discussions—and almost none among groups of struggling readers—involved questions that did not have a predetermined correct answer (Nystrand, 1999). In a more recent study, Smith, Hardman, Wall, and Mroz (2004) analyzed 100 classrooms and found that 70% of student responses involved three words or less!

We do know that carefully structured talk can enhance reading comprehension and learning in general. Also called *analytic talk, literate talk*, or *dialogic instruction*, effective dialogue engages learners in extended and purposeful conversations to construct meaning, clarify thinking, and collaboratively build new ideas. The teacher's role is to carefully scaffold that discussion, injecting new information as needed, but, more importantly, supporting students as they figure things out on their own. Too often, we've assumed that our struggling readers are not capable of higher-level talk. Yet talking to learn may very well be more appropriate for struggling learners than for anyone else, as it prompts, supports, and scaffolds them as they collaboratively sort out their own thinking. Dialogic instruction is cooperative, not competitive. Students learn, not just to articulate their thinking, but also to listen to others, to allow others time to organize their thinking, to respect alternative points of view, and to express ideas clearly and courteously.

Although teacher talk is reduced in this type of instructional situation, teachers continue to have a very important role in modeling language, inserting guiding questions, and encouraging students to elaborate and explain their thinking. Carefully crafted teacher interactions can inject new ideas, prompt extended thinking, and model appropriate language and behaviors.

There are a number of ways we can adapt existing classroom conversational practices to make them more effective tools for supporting literacy and learning:

What We Tend to Do	What We Can do Better
Assume that students know the norms and behaviors of literate talk and focus only on the content of the discussion.	Model, demonstrate, and practice behaviors of taking turns, asking questions, allowing others time to think and elaborate, stating ideas clearly, and disagreeing politely.
Ask a lot of questions that require brief, right-or-wrong answers.	Craft our prompts and questions to raise the length and level of student responses.
Accept superficial or unsupported responses.	Always encourage elaboration and/or support for thinking.
Expect immediate responses; recognize those who raise their hands or call out most quickly.	Give students the time they need to formulate their ideas and to elaborate on their responses; use wait time both before and after responding.
Fill silences with teacher talk.	Get comfortable with silences for thinking, reflecting, and processing ideas.
Respond with vague praise such as "Good" or "Mmmm."	Avoid passing value judgments on responses; instead, restate key ideas and probe further.
Use the same vocabulary as the students.	Incorporate more complex vocabulary and sentence structure into prompting, restating, or responding.

Think–Pair–Share

The problem with any kind of group discussion is that it's easy for one or two students to dominate the conversation and for others to disengage entirely. As teachers, we need a system for ensuring that everyone has an equal opportunity—and responsibility—to participate in the discussion. Think–Pair–Share was developed many years ago by Frank Lyman (1981) as a way to involve all students in classroom discussion.

The think–pair–share structure has three parts:

Think: Reflect on your own ideas
Pair: Discuss your ideas with a partner
Share: Bring your thoughts to the group

Alternatives to think–pair–share include think–pair–draw–share or think–pair–write–share.

1. Students are given a brief time (less than a minute) to individually reflect on a problem or question.
2. They discuss these thoughts with a partner for a longer time.
3. They have an opportunity to share their ideas with a larger group.

Sometimes we might have pairs combine into groups of four for sharing; at other times we might invite specific individuals to share their ideas; and sometimes we might not move into large-group sharing at all, if it seems that the paired discussion has been adequate.

I use this protocol, which I call Talk To Your Neighbor or TTYN, as a standard routine for any higher-level discussion. The research on think–pair–share shows that this structure increases student participation in discussions and increases the level of their thinking (Lyman, 1981). It addresses the needs of those who need a few minutes to compose their thoughts before articulating them, as well as the needs of those who need to talk through their thinking. It is particularly important for struggling readers to have an opportunity to organize, rehearse, and try out their thinking before sharing it publicly—and it doesn't hurt for other students either. In fact, Lyman's research suggests that this routine increases both participation and higher-level thinking for all students. The added benefit is that large-group discussions are more focused and efficient.

Organizing Partner Talk

In pairing students for TTYN (Talk To Your Neighbor) or Think–Pair–Share, find a system that works for you and is quick, efficient, and random. Don't leave it up to students to choose partners and don't bother trying to match students of similar reading levels. I use a system of *partner sticks*, or craft sticks with colored dots at the bottom. Each student draws a partner stick at random and is automatically paired with the person who has the stick with the same-colored dot. (You can do the same thing by randomly dealing from a deck of playing cards.) Pairing students in this way allow them to experience working with a range of different partners, and no one gets left out.

Prompts for Thinking Aloud

- This reminds me of…

- In my background knowledge, I know…

- I'm predicting that…

- I'm inferring that…

- I'm wondering…

- Why is/why did…

- Should/shouldn't there be…?

- What happened to…?

- I was/wasn't expecting…

- I can just picture…

- I'm a little confused here…

- I'm not sure of…

- The key idea here is…

- This is worth remembering, I think:…

- I think that the author…

- I need to go back and reread that part…

- Remember when it said…

- I love the way the author…

- I was thinking that…but now I'm thinking that…

- The most important message here is…

© 2014 *Struggling Readers* by Lori Jamison Rog. Pembroke Publishers. ISBN 978-1-55138-292-0

5

Struggling Readers Need Comprehension Superpowers

Our students live in a world filled with stories of superheroes. From TVs to T-shirts, young people are inundated with images and tales of Superman, Spider-man, Wonder Woman, Batman, and the X-Men—human beings with superhuman powers. Comprehension strategies are the superpowers that enable readers to transform those little marks on the page into words and ideas. And the good news is that it doesn't take exposure to kryptonite or cosmic rays to create super readers. It does take instruction, practice, and an awareness of the reading process.

There is no consensus among reading experts as to which reading strategies are most important. The preceding chapter lists several strategies identified by David Pearson and Nell Duke in their seminal research on comprehension (2002). Anne-Marie Palincsar and Ann Brown, in their well-documented Reciprocal Teaching model, emphasize four: questioning, clarifying, summarizing, and predicting. Pearson and Duke remind us that metacognitive use of even one strategy aids comprehension; however, strategy use is more effective if strategies are taught and practiced in combinations. In my work with struggling readers, I focus on what I call the Fab Four superpowers of reading: asking questions during reading, drawing inferences, self-monitoring comprehension, and pulling it all together, or synthesizing.

Asking oneself questions during reading requires the reader to actively engage with text, monitor comprehension, and set purposes for reading. Inferring, or reading between the lines, involves making connections to one's own background knowledge in order to fill in understandings that are not directly stated in the text. Self-monitoring demands that readers constantly pay attention to whether or not they understand what they are reading, then apply strategies to fix up any mix-ups. Synthesizing is defined as combining parts into a connected whole; in terms of reading, it involves pulling together the pieces to come to an overall understanding. Synthesizing requires readers to integrate all the other reading superpowers.

Of course, if we had an ultimate superhero of reading, it would have to be Metacognition Man. Metacognition is, essentially, thinking about our thinking. Effective strategy use requires metacognitive awareness of the reading process. As long as our reading is easy or going well, we don't pay a lot of attention to what we're doing as readers. But when we hit a point of confusion in our reading, we need to take deliberate action. Metacognition Man to the rescue! Metacognition guides us in choosing and using the superpowers we need to repair our misunderstandings and correct our confusions.

Strategic Choice of Text

It's important to remember that effective strategy use is contingent upon reading appropriate-level texts. If the reading is too difficult, students will be unable to apply their strategies; if the reading is easy, strategies are unnecessary. Just because a reader has mastered a strategy at one level, it doesn't mean that he/she won't need more practice in the strategy at higher levels. Finding the texts that keep readers on their toes is the best way to take every student from where he/she is to where he/she can be (see page 13).

Sticky Notes for Active Reading

All too often, our struggling learners view reading as something that just happens—or doesn't happen, as the case may be. They don't realize that reading is an active process that requires readers to be constantly aware of what they are thinking and doing, and of what they need to think and do to make sense of the text. One way to help readers build that metacognitive capacity is to have them use sticky notes to track their thinking as they read.

When we invite students to mark points of interest in the text and note their questions, confusions, connections, disagreements, or delights in what they read, we are teaching them to be engaged, reflective readers. Tracking thinking with sticky notes requires readers to think about what the text says and means, and to draw on their reading superpowers. And most importantly, it builds readers who are active participants in, not passive recipients of, the reading process. That's what metacognition is all about.

A word of caution: many of our struggling readers have already been peppered with paper in previous grades and may not be as motivated to track their thinking with sticky notes as we are. Sticky-note tracking should serve specific purposes and be as authentic as it's possible to be in a classroom situation. We can keep sticky-note reading fresh by using different sizes, shapes, and colors of notes, by using them in a variety of ways, and by always ensuring that students see the purpose for using them. We need to show our students how metacognition makes them better readers and, as always, to build successes while supporting students as they grow.

Using sticky notes to track thinking during reading is not an end in itself; it is a means to an end. In small-group guided reading, we guide, support, and scaffold students in identifying and articulating the strategies they use so that they will be able to apply those superpowers both automatically and intentionally in their independent reading. The ultimate goal is for students to have a repertoire of tools in their reading toolbox to apply when comprehension breaks down. Sticky-note reading is one way to fill that toolbox.

The Reading Toolkit

One of the challenges of sticky-note reading is managing all those little scraps of paper. In a brief small-group reading lesson, we simply don't want to waste time searching for or distributing sticky notes. My simple and inexpensive solution is the Reading Toolkit, a folder stocked with sticky notes that enables us to have these tools at hand and use them quickly and efficiently. Sometimes I provide a variety of stickies from which students can choose, and other times I will have the toolkits pre-stocked with the specific size or type of sticky notes that will be needed for that day's reading.

Reading Toolkits are easy to create from a colored file folder. With the file folder closed, cut it in 3" (10 cm) folded strips. This gives you four Toolkits from one file folder. Add a label, if you choose, and laminate the unfolded Toolkit for durability. Refold and add a plastic coil for a small pencil at the top (the small pencils that go with your golf scorecard work well). Now you're set to stock the Toolkit with sticky notes for active reading.

Tools for Sticky-Note Reading
- various sizes, colors, and shapes of sticky notes
- sticky-note Stop Sign to indicate stopping points
- highlighting tape
- colored flags
- pencil or pen

 ## Comprehension Superpower: Asking Questions During Reading

"When students generate their own questions, they become actively engaged in reading and motivated by their own queries rather than those of the teacher." National Reading Panel (2000)

As good readers, we wonder all the time. Sometimes we wonder why a character acted as he/she did or what he/she might do next. Sometimes we wonder why an author chose to include a particular detail, or whether a new clue will help solve a mystery. Sometimes we wonder what a cryptic newspaper headline is all about or what a politician has done to get his/her picture in the paper yet again. Sometimes we simply wonder about the meaning of an unfamiliar word or unusual turn of phrase. Whether reading a novel, a textbook, or an e-mail, asking themselves questions helps readers set purposes for reading, monitor their own comprehension, and generally engage more actively in the reading process. The routines that follow provide guided practice in wondering during reading, turning those "wonderings" into questions, and increasing awareness of how readers find answers to those questions.

The Language of Questioning
- *I wonder…*
- *Why did…?*
- *What will…?*
- *Who could…?*
- *Which one…?*

⟶ *I Wonder/I Think/I Know*

Students will be able to track their wonderings as they read and to identify them as literal or inferential.

Remind students that wondering supports reading in three main ways: wondering helps us think about what the reading means and whether the reading is making sense; it also helps set purposes for reading, as we have to read on to find answers to our wonderings; perhaps most importantly, it can lead us deeper into the text, drawing our attention to things we might not have noticed otherwise.

1. Choose an appropriate text and plan pause points every few paragraphs.
2. Have students individually read the first section of text and instruct them to reflect on what they wonder as they read it. You might have them tab a couple of wonder points with sticky notes or tell them to hold their ideas in their heads until everyone completes the brief reading. (Faster readers can go back and reread the text while they wait.)
3. After reading, have students share their wonderings with a partner and discuss what they think the answers to their wonderings might be.
4. Invite the pairs to share some of their wonderings with the whole group. Record some of the students' wonderings on a chart to set a purpose for further reading, as students must read on to look for the answers to their wonderings.
5. Now have students read the next section of text, both to look for answers to their previous wonderings and to reflect on new wonderings.
6. As you discuss this reading, ask students whether any of the previous wonderings were answered. Talk about whether the information was stated directly (*I Know*) or if readers had to figure out the answers from clues in the text (*I Think*). If the answers are *I Think*, then students should be asked to identify the clues in the text that support the inference.
7. Add additional wonderings to the group chart and continue reading to the next pause point. Continue this process to the end of the passage or the end of the lesson.

Must-Do Practice

Have students read a section of accessible text (such as another excerpt from the same text as the lesson) and tab three or four points of wonder, writing their wonderings on sticky notes. At the next small-group lesson, invite a discussion of the wonderings and what the students anticipate the answers will be. Students might be asked to create a two-column chart to record their *I Wonder*s and record what they *think* or what they *know* the answer to each one might be.

From Wonderings to Questions

Students will be able to convert "I wonder" statements into questions.

In the previous lesson routine, the words *wonderings* and *questions* are used interchangeably. However, some of our struggling learners might not understand the grammatical distinction between an *I Wonder* statement and a question. You might want to take a few minutes to assess this understanding and, if necessary, spend some time modeling and practicing converting statements to questions. For example, we can teach students to take the statement "I wonder if the boys will continue to be friends" and flip it to "Will the boys continue to be friends?"

Must-Do Practice

Repeat the must-do from the preceding routine, I Wonder/I Think/I Know (page 49), in which students tab three or four points of wonder. This time, have students record their wonderings as questions on the sticky notes.

Question-Grid Game Show

Students will be able to recognize, generate, and answer different types of questions.

> **The Question Grid**
>
> The question grid is a tool for generating different types of questions. The version of the chart on page 65 includes these question starters: *Who, What, When/Where* (pertaining to setting), *Why, How,* and *Which* (generating questions that require a choice). The verbs on the horizontal row of the grid lend themselves to increasingly complex questions as you move from left to right. For example, *is/are/was/were* and *does/did* are verbs that generally lend themselves to literal-level questions; for example, "Who was Wilbur's best friend?" or "Where did Charlotte write her messages?" Using verbs *will, would/should/could,* and *might* generates higher-level thinking by inviting prediction and speculation; for example, "What might happen the next time Mr. Arable has a runt pig?" or "What should Wilbur do with Charlotte's babies?"

1. If your struggling readers are unfamiliar with these question structures, start with only the first column of the grid on page 65 and work on *who, what, when/where, which,* and *why* questions. Have students take turns asking and answering questions about a common text that has been read. Gradually introduce the next three vertical columns, and then the final three columns, to practice generating questions.

You can make your own game dice out of milk cartons. Clean the milk cartons and cut them down so the height is equal to the length and width (i.e., cube-sized). Tuck one carton bottom inside the other to form a cube with all six sides solid. Cover the cube with paper and add labels.

2. When students are comfortable with developing questions, use the question grid as a game-show board. Create two dice, one with the six interrogatives and one with the six sets of verbs.
3. Make two teams and have them take turns rolling the dice and generating questions using the words that come up. Write each question in the appropriate square on the grid.
4. The other team has an opportunity to answer the question. If they can answer it, the square goes to their team; if not, the questioning team must be able to answer their own question and get the square. Teacher is the final arbiter (of course) of whether a question or an answer is legitimate.
5. If a team member rolls a combination that is already on the board, that player can choose which of the dice to roll again. If the player again gets a combination that's taken, he/she forfeits the turn.

These rules are just suggestions. Teachers can to make up their own rules for the game.

6. The team with the most squares to their credit when the board is full (or the time is up) is the winner.

Must-Do Practice

Provide each pair of students with a set of dice to roll and take turns developing questions about a common text. One student makes up a question and the other must answer it. If you would like a product for assessment, have the students create individual question cards with the questions on one side and the answers on the other. At the next meeting of the group, you can place all the questions in a gift bag for students in the group to take turns drawing a card at random and trying to answer the question.

Hand, Head, and Heart Questions

Students will be able to identify literal, inferential, and affective/evaluative questions.

It's important for readers to know not just what the answer to a question is, but how they arrived at that answer. Metacognition Man in action!

Remind students that sometimes the answer is right there in front of us on the page. In fact, we could put a *hand* right on the information. Sometimes the answers aren't right there, but the author gives us enough clues to enable us to use our *heads* to figure out the answers. Sometimes, however, there aren't any clues at all, and the only way to figure out the answer is to draw on the feelings, experiences, or background knowledge inside us, in our *hearts*. We can identify these three types of questions as Hand, Head, and Heart questions.

The ability to indentify literal, inferential, and affective questions will help students get credit for what they know on large-scale reading tests, because this knowledge guides them in knowing how and where to look for the answers.

1. Review some questions from the Question-Grid Game Show grid (see page 50) and have students identify them as *Hand*, *Head*, or *Heart* questions.
2. Have students practice generating the three different types of questions orally from a familiar text. Teachers should be prepared with some questions as well. You will probably find that generating Hand and Heart questions is not that difficult for most students, but Head questions are more challenging (even for teachers). The difference between Heart and Head questions is found in the text support. Remember that there must be some clues to draw on from the text in order to answer inferential questions.
3. Students take turns responding to the questions generated. When they answer Hand questions, they should scan for the information in the text. When they respond to Head questions, they should provide supporting clues from the text. When they answer Heart questions, they should tell what background knowledge they have to support their response.

Hand/Head/Heart Questions

Hand questions	Who/What/When/Where?	*Literal* information: the answer is directly stated in the text
Head questions	Why do you think…? What do you predict/infer?	*Inferential* information: the answer is a combination of clues from the text and the reader's background knowledge
Heart questions	How would you feel if…? What would you do if…? What connections do you make…?	*Affective* or *evaluative* information: the answer comes from the reader's own feelings, experience, or background knowledge

Provide students with lots of guided practice before expecting them to be able to develop these questions on their own. In truth, it's more important that our struggling readers be able to identify and respond to these questions than it is that they be able to create them from scratch.

Must-Do Practice

Have students create a three-column flap book (see directions below) or use the graphic organizer on page 66, folded in half. On the outside, write one Hand question, one Heart question, and one Head question from independent reading or teacher-assigned text. Under each flap, the student writes the answer to the question.

Folded Flap Book

Lift-the-flap books can have as many flaps as you choose. These instructions are for three flaps.

1. Fold a piece of paper in half lengthwise (hotdog fold).
2. Then fold it in three crosswise (hamburger) folds, so that the paper is folded in six.
3. Unfold the crosswise folds, leaving one fold and three creases. Place the paper in front of you with the long fold at the top and the opening at the bottom.
4. Cut each top crease only to the centre fold, so that the bottom is one solid piece and the top consists of three flaps.
5. The flap book can be used horizontally or vertically.

Comprehension Superpower: Inferring

One of the essential superpowers of reading is the ability to understand and interpret ideas that are not directly stated by the author—in other words, to infer. The author gives us some information and we need to draw on our own background knowledge to supply the missing information. Remind students that an inference is a new idea that the reader thinks is probably true about the reading, based on clues that the author gives combined with information that the reader already knows.

Here's the good news: even our struggling readers already know how to infer. They draw inferences all the time—about reading, movies, TV, and even other people. Your students are quick to judge whether you are happy or annoyed by the expression on your face and the tone of your voice. They can determine whether or not it's safe to cross the road. They can decide whether to bring an umbrella or sunglasses to school. The bad news is that most of our struggling readers are not aware of what they're doing when they infer; in other words, they're not metacognitive about it. Why is this important? When the reading is easy, inference is automatic. But when the reading gets difficult, it's important to be able to intentionally and purposefully select a superpower like inference to help make the connections between background knowledge and text clues in order to make sense of the reading. That's where metacognition comes in.

The lesson routines in this section start with using pictures and simple text to help students understand what inference is, why it's important, and how they can use it. Then we'll move on to more challenging routines in which students must negotiate text and identify the inferences they make as they read.

You Infer All the Time

Sample Text for Inferring

Students will be able to recognize the process of inferring during reading.

> I told my brother I would take him because he was too young to get in by himself. When we got to the counter, I gave the man a twenty and he gave me two tickets and four dollars change. My brother wanted to pay me back but I told him to buy the popcorn instead.

1. Enlarge the sample text to display to the class and read it aloud to/with the students.

2. Invite them to TTYN (Talk To Your Neighbor) about what the text is about. If necessary, prompt with questions:
   - *Where were they going?*
   - *Which sibling is older?*
   - *How much did it cost?*
   - *What is a twenty?*
   - *What is a counter? (Someone who counts?)*
   - *Who is "he" in "he was too young"? Who is "he" in "he gave me two tickets"?*
3. As students share ideas about the text, keep asking them to explain how they know. Draw their attention to information that wasn't stated, but that readers had to fill in; for example, that a "twenty" is a twenty-dollar bill and a "counter" in this case is like a table or shelf.
4. Remind the students that making "educated guesses" like this is actually a reading superpower called inferring. Explain: "When we read, we often have to use our background knowledge to *infer* information that is implied, but not directly stated in the text." Talk about the process of deciding that certain ideas from the text are probably true because of what the author said and what the reader already knows.
5. Explain to students that often we infer without even thinking about it. But when the reading gets tough, it's important to stop and use our superpowers to think about what clues the author is giving us and what we have to figure out on our own.

Must-Do Practice

Provide pairs of students with riddle cards from page 67 to practice drawing inferences. There are four clues on each card. Partners take turns reading one clue at a time, while the other partner guesses. Have students create their own riddles.

Making Connections to Prior Knowledge

Students will be able to identify background knowledge needed to draw inferences and make sense of text.

An important part of the inference superpower is the ability to draw on one's own background knowledge. Many struggling readers lack the necessary background knowledge to make sense of what they read in school, or they don't know how to intentionally access and apply the background knowledge they have. There are different ways that readers develop prior knowledge; where the knowledge comes from is less important than recognizing and using the information base, or schema (a cognitive framework that helps us organize information around us). However, it helps students to be more metacognitive readers if they are aware of connecting what they read to personal experience (text-to-self connections), to other reading (text-to-text connections), or to general knowledge (text-to-world connections).

The Language of Connecting
- *This reminds me of…*
- *This is like…*
- *I'm making a connection to…*
- *I already know…*
- *This connection helped me understand the text because…*

1. Choose an appropriate text and plan pause points every few paragraphs.
2. Have students individually read the first section of text and instruct them to reflect on what connections they made as they read it. You might have them use sticky notes to tab a couple of connections or tell them to hold their ideas in their heads until everyone completes the brief reading. (Faster readers can go back and reread the text while they wait.)
3. After reading, have students share their connections with a partner and discuss whether the connections are text-to-self, text-to-text, or text-to-world.
4. Invite pairs to share some of their connections with the whole group. Take note of how different readers make different connections and how this might affect their understanding of and response to what they read.
5. Have students read the next section of text, thinking individually about their connections, then share with a partner.
6. As you discuss this reading, invite students to think about how their connections helped (or didn't help) them understand the text and draw inferences.
7. Continue this process to the end of the passage or the end of the lesson.

Must-Do Practice

Provide students with sticky notes and an accessible text; have them note three or four places they made connections and how these connections related to their understanding of the text.

The Inference Formula

Students will be able to understand that inference involves combining textual information with background knowledge.

Remind students that inferring is interpreting ideas by filling in gaps in information from one's own personal knowledge. In this lesson, students take a look at the process of inferring; in other words, the inference formula.

1. Provide students with a simple statement such as this one:

   Sally blew out the candles and opened her presents.

2. Ask students what they can infer about this statement. (It's Sally's birthday, of course.) How do you know? (You read that she blew out candles and opened presents, and you know that candles and presents go with a birthday celebration, so you inferred that it's Sally's birthday.) Here's the formula:

   What you read + what you know = what you infer

3. Create a chart like the one on the next page and have students practice working through, or unpacking, simple inferences.
4. Have students TTYN (Talk To Your Neighbor) to discuss the inferences generated by each of the statements in the chart.
5. Collaboratively complete the chart by identifying the background knowledge needed to draw these inferences. Discuss the fact that different people might come up with different inferences based on their own background knowledge and interpretation of the text.

Sample Inference Formula Chart

What You Read	*What You Know*	*What You Infer*
Sally blew out the candles and opened presents.	*You blow out candles on a cake and receive presents on your birthday.*	*It must be Sally's birthday.*
When I woke up in the morning, the yard was filled with broken branches and leaves.		
Everyone stopped skating when the referee blew the whistle.		
Yesterday, we cleaned out our desks and said good-bye to the teacher.		

Must-Do Practice

Provide each pair of students with an Inference Formula Chart graphic organizer (see page 68) and statements like the ones below. Have them complete the chart by identifying the inference and the background knowledge required to get it.

Sample Statements

- The girls put on their swimsuits and got out their towels.
- I put my airline ticket and my passport in my bag.
- The dog stuck one paw out the door, shivered, and ran back inside the house.
- "Simon is a pretty good pitcher but he acts like his hand is made of glass. (from *Baseball Bats* by Sharon Jennings)
- "We all chipped in when Hammy's line drive smashed Mrs. Headly's window." (from *Ghost House* by Paul Kropp)

Inferring from Pictures

Students will be able to apply their understanding of the inference process to visual cues.

In this lesson, students will practice their metacognitive skills by drawing inferences from pictures.

1. Reproduce the photo on page 69 or another picture of your choice.
2. Using the prompts on page 69, invite students to draw inferences about what might have happened just before the picture and what might happen right after. Always focus on noting specific details from the picture and drawing on the requisite background knowledge that leads to the inferences.

Must-Do Practice

Provide pairs of students with sets of pictures and Inference Formula Chart graphic organizers on which to record inferences about the pictures and the details and background knowledge that support those inferences.

A 2011 book entitled *The Chronicles of Harris Burdick* contains 14 stories. Based on the original pictures from *The Mysteries of Harris Burdick*, the stories are written by well-known authors from the worlds of both children's and adult literature.

Students will be able to identify the inferences required to appreciate humor in cartoons.

Finding Pictures for Practicing Inferences

Google images can provide good sources of pictures: an Internet search, such as "naughty children" or "funny animals," will turn up many images that will engage students and inspire inferences. (One of my favorites is a toddler who has just written all over her baby sibling's head with colored markers.)

Another good source of interesting pictures from which to practice inferences is *The Mysteries of Harris Burdick* by Chris van Allsburg. This old picture book—probably already in your school library—consists of several unusual images, each accompanied by a title and a single line of text, which compel readers to draw inferences about what is happening.

Inferring from Cartoons and Comic Strips

A cartoon from the comic strip *Rhymes with Orange* by Hilary Price depicts two caterpillars on a leaf. As they look over at another caterpillar and a butterfly perched together on a nearby flower, one says to the other, "Look who's got himself a cougar." What makes this cartoon humorous? Well, you need the pop culture reference to a "cougar" as an older woman who dates younger men. As well, you need to know that the caterpillar and butterfly are the same creature, with the butterfly being a later stage of maturity; in other words, the butterfly is the "older woman" of the insect world. The cartoonist gives us some information in pictures and words, but we need to fill in the gaps from our background knowledge in order to understand the humor. Humor is full of inference—which is one reason why our struggling readers often just don't get it. Cartoons and comic strips can be terrifically engaging tools for helping students unpack the inferences that lead to humor.

1. Gather a collection of student-friendly (appropriate and accessible) cartoons from newspapers or the Internet.
2. Tell students that writers of comics assume that readers have certain background knowledge that will be required to understand the joke. Talk to the students about the importance of activating background knowledge to appreciate cartoons, and how, if a reader doesn't have the appropriate background knowledge, the reader is likely to miss the point of the joke.
3. Modify the Inference Formula Chart on page 68 so the first column head is *I read/view*. Use the chart to collaboratively record the information provided in the visuals and text of the cartoon, the background knowledge necessary, and the ultimate inferences required to access the intended humor.
4. As students become familiar with the practice, invite them to search for their own cartoons to share with the class. You'll want to set some criteria, not the least of which is appropriateness for school consumption, and including the requirement that the student who brings the cartoon must be able to explain "what I read, what I know, and what I infer."

Must-Do Practice

Provide each pair of students with two or three cartoons and a Inference Formula Chart (page 68) to analyze each of the jokes. You might choose to have students record the information on the chart or have them simply discuss with a partner and be able to share their inferences at the next group meeting.

What's Your Inference?

It's one thing to be able to draw inferences from pictures, stories, and other texts that are read aloud; it's quite another to infer while in the process of navigating print. Struggling readers need plenty of practice reading extended text and thinking about their thinking as they read. After you have done a lot of modeling and demonstration through think-alouds, and have invited students to think along in pairs or individually, it's time to give them opportunities to think alone as they read.

1. Carefully choose a text at an appropriate reading difficulty for the group, one that lends itself to inference and stretches the students just slightly beyond their current reading level. Plan four or five strategic pause points where inferences are necessary to understand the text.
2. Have students read to the first pause point, then stop and talk to a partner about the inferences they made as they read.
3. Invite the pairs to share their inferences with the whole group. Have students identify the cues in the text and the background knowledge necessary to understand the inference.
4. Continue with each of the pause points, discussing the inferences in pairs and small groups. Students may be encouraged to use one of the inference sentence stems from The Language of Inference box.

The Language of Inference
- *I'm inferring that…*
- *I think that…because…*
- *I predict…*
- *I interpret that…*
- *I'm guessing… because…*
- *I'm concluding…*
- *I figured out that…*
- *I assume that…because…*

Must-Do Practice

If possible, provide students with a practice text that has thinking boxes inserted at key inference points (see sample on page 58), or have students place sticky notes at several predetermined pause points. Instruct students to read independently, pausing when they encounter a thinking box or pause point to record their inferences. Remind students that they will be expected to share their reasoning for each inference when the group reconvenes.

As students build confidence in identifying and explaining their inferences, provide appropriate texts without predetermined pause points. Have students use sticky notes to mark and record places where they had to draw inferences. At the next group session, take time to discuss the students' inferences and the reading process.

Sample Text with Thinking Boxes

Sample text is an excerpt from *The Crash* by Paul Kropp.

Lost in the Snow

Rory just lay in the snow. This was bad. When you get really frozen, you start to give up like that. You shiver and get dizzy and give up. And then you freeze to death.

> *I'm inferring that…*

So I bent over him and grabbed his sleeves. "Get up, you jerk," I shouted at him. "I can see the house!" That was a lie, but I had to do something.

> *I'm inferring that…*

"You can?" Rory asked.

"Yeah, just come with me," I told him.

So I got Rory moving again – with a lie. There was no light up ahead. But I knew we had to keep moving. If we just lay down, we'd be dead.

"We're almost there," I said, lying some more.

Rory didn't speak. We just kept moving forward – towards nothing. The snow swirled in the wind. The dark night made the world all black with white flecks. There was nothing – nothing at all.

Until I saw a dark shape.

> *I'm inferring that…*

What a Character!

Students will be able to draw inferences about characters in their reading from what the character says and does, and from what others say about the character.

There are three ways that readers learn about characters in novels and storybooks: by what the author says about them, by what they say and do, and by what others say about them. In this lesson, students will practice drawing inferences about characters by reading connected text.

1. With students, examine a piece of text that focuses on a character (see below for an example). Invite students to talk about what they can infer about the character from what he/she does and says.

Sample Inference about a Character

Sample text is from *Ghost House* by Paul Kropp.

Hammy zoomed up the sidewalk to the steps then did a 180 Ollie that looked pretty slick. "Hey, ghosts!" he shouted. "How do you like that? You want to see me do a grind?"

> *We have to have some background knowledge to know that a 180 Ollie is a skateboarding move. Obviously Hammy is a pretty good skateboarder and a bit of a show-off from the way he shouts at the ghosts, "How do you like that?"*

2. Use other short samples of text, such as those below, to continue to practise inferring about characters. Always require that students explain the text cues and necessary background knowledge to support the inference.

Hero hunched down and whimpered. His eyes showed a sliver of white as he gazed to one side. It was a look of pure terror. There on the fence sat a huge, shaggy, gray animal. "Meet Killer the Cat," grinned Mario. (from *Dog on Trial* by Sylvia McNicoll)

Frank's always pushing me to do stuff and try things. He's the guy who plays out on the ice flows during the spring melt. He's the guy who kicks at Snarly Joe's dogs. He's the guy who gets in trouble. (from *Frozen* by Lori Jamison)

Must-Do Practice

Provide students with an accessible text excerpt that describes one or more characters; the sample chapter from Ghost House in Appendix A (page 142) would work well. Then have them use the Character Chart graphic organizer on page 136 to identify character traits and the evidence from the text that supports them.

Predicting: Seeing the Future

Predicting is a part of the inferring superpower because it requires readers to combine clues from the text with background knowledge to anticipate what will come next in the reading. The important thing about prediction as a reading strategy is that it is an ongoing process. It's difficult to convince students that there's no glory in predicting the entire story from the cover or first few pages of a book! If you can do that, why bother reading the rest of the book? Good readers are constantly confirming or adjusting their predictions based on new information in their reading. This is a powerful lesson for struggling readers, who often assume they are the only ones who can't seem to guess what's going to happen next or can't put together the clues to a mystery.

That doesn't mean that any old guess makes a good prediction. A prediction is an educated guess, based on information in the text. Predicting from the cover or back-cover blurb doesn't contribute much to the reading process. Have students read a section of text, look at the table of contents, or preview some illustrations to activate background knowledge before inviting them to predict what will happen.

What Happens Next?

Students will be able to construct ongoing predictions that are supported by text.

It's counter-productive to record students' predictions; the whole point is for them to change or adjust them as necessary.

1. Select an accessible passage for the group to read and plan two or three pause points that lend themselves to prediction.
2. Have students place a sticky-note Stop Sign at the first pause point and read silently and independently to that point, reflecting on their prediction of what will happen next. It's often helpful, especially with struggling readers, to guide thinking with a prompt or question to help them focus their predictions: *What do you think this character will do next?* helps focus a prediction better than *What do you think will happen next?*
3. Have students talk to a partner (or think–pair–share) about their predictions and the textual evidence behind them. It might be necessary to remind students that their predictions might turn out to be wrong, but that the important thing is that the predictions are supported by information in the reading.

4. After discussing the first prediction, have students move their sticky notes to the next pause point and repeat the process.

5. After the reading is complete, discuss with the students how predicting helped (or didn't help) them as readers.

Must-Do Practice

Provide each student with an accessible reading passage pre-marked with two or three prediction pause points. Ideally, reproduce the text with thinking boxes (two columns, labeled "I predict…" and "because…") already inserted. However, large sticky notes placed at strategic spots before reading will also work for students to record their predictions and supporting evidence. Don't be surprised if students read on before recording their predictions. After all, our struggling readers have spent their school careers trying to avoid being publicly "wrong." It may not be an all-bad thing, as they will have to be pretty strategic about searching for support for their predictions from each section of text.

Comprehension Superpower: Monitoring and Clarifying Comprehension

Talk to Your Brain is a metaphor for the self-talk that readers do to monitor their own comprehension.

Probably the most significant difference between effective and ineffective readers is the ability to monitor one's own comprehension. Good readers sometimes make miscues, encounter points of confusion, or just plain don't get it. But good readers usually know when they've hit a snag and have both the confidence and competence to repair the problem. Unfortunately, many of our struggling readers don't even know when they don't get it. They keep plugging along without attending to whether their reading is making sense. And if they do recognize a break in their comprehension, they lack both the skill and the will to repair it. Our challenge is to help our struggling readers develop the superpower to recognize comprehension difficulties and use their strategies to fix up their mix-ups.

The Language of Self-Monitoring
- *This isn't clear to me.*
- *I don't get this…*
- *I'm not sure what this means.*
- *I think I'd better read this section again.*
- *I hit a "clunk" here, so here's what I did…*

Remote-Control Reading

Students will be able to pause regularly to self-monitor comprehension.

Teach students to think of using the remote control to watch a movie on TV as a metaphor for reading. Just as we press the *Play* button to start our show, we press the *Play* button in our brains to start reading.

1. Explain to students that every now and then (let's say, every page) when we're reading, we need to hit the *Pause* button in our brains and ask ourselves, "Is this making sense to me? Do I understand all of this? What did I just read?"

2. If we answer ourselves, "Yes, this makes sense!" then we hit that mental *Play* button again and keep on reading.
3. If the answer to ourselves is "No," then we need to hit the Stop button in our brains and either Rewind or Fast Forward to use our strategies to fix up the mix-up.

Must-Do Practice

Buttons on the Reading Remote Control
▸ Play
Ⅱ Pause
■ Stop
◂◂ Rewind
▸▸ Fast Forward

Provide students with their own reading remote-controls to remind them to pause and self-monitor as they read. Some teachers provide each student with a bookmark labeled with the remote-control symbols. But it's easy to find inexpensive remote-control devices at your local dollar store. In this way, fidgeters can actually feel like they are physically hitting the buttons as they use their mental clickers.

Clicks and Clunks

Students will be able to identify points of confusion in their reading.

When reading is going well, everything just *clicks*. But every now and then, we hit a *clunk*—a point of confusion or misunderstanding. Good readers hit clunks all the time, but we fix them up and get clicking again. One of the challenges for struggling readers is that they don't always know when they've hit a clunk and, if they do know, they don't know what do about it. The term *clicks and clunks* (Klingner & Vaughn, 1998) is powerful because it suggests that trouble with a text is a temporary setback to be corrected so that the reader can move on.

1. Stock the Reading Toolkits with red and green flags.
2. Choose a piece of text that is likely to contain two or three points of confusion; alternatively, doctor a piece of text to add points of confusion (see example on page 62).
3. Tell students that they are to pay careful attention to whether their reading is making sense to them, as they click along. When they come to a clunk, or place when comprehension breaks down, they are to tab it with a red flag (like a stop light).
4. If they are able to use their strategies to fix up their confusion, they replace the red flag with a green one (to get clicking again).
5. After reading each section of text, stop to discuss the points at which students hit clunks in the reading, what fix-up strategies they used, and what strategies they might use another time. It is often useful to reframe these fix-up strategies as "I can" statements and maintain an anchor chart of Fix-Up-the-Mix-up Tools.

Must-Do Practice

Provide students with a piece of text that is mostly accessible, but that you know contains two or three points of confusion. The sample "The Bully" has a mid-Grade 3 reading level, but has been altered to include at least five points that don't make sense. Invite students to read and tab the points of confusion with red flags. After reading, talk about the *clunks* and correct the confusing information.

Reading level: Grade 2. Sample adapted from *The Bully* by Liz Brown; used with permission from High Interest Publishing.

The Bully

Danni began to bully me back in Grade 7. That was four years ago. It still gives me shivers when I think back. Danni Heller was the worst bully in our school—and he was a girl.

You read about *boy* bullies all the time. You hear how they choose a victim. How they choose some kid who's smaller and weaker than they are. How they dress in fancy clothes. How they pick on the kid, day after day. You hear about all the physical stuff—the pushes, the punches, the kicks.

But girl bullies aren't like that. A girl bully won't beat you up. Instead, she beats up your brain. She makes you so scared that you wake up each day just ready to laugh.

I know—I was the victim.

It didn't make sense when it all started. Danni and I had been good friends when we were little. But then Katie moved in across the street and she was a lot more fun to be with. Maybe Danni didn't like that. Maybe she was jealous. Maybe she thought that Katie and I wanted to be friends with her. Or maybe I'm just blaming myself. They say victims do that. We blame ourselves for what the bully does.

Fix-Up Tools

The first part of the self-monitoring superpower is recognizing points of confusion; the next part is fixing up those mix-ups. Most of our struggling readers have a limited repertoire of fix-up tools; they are likely to either keep reading, even when they don't comprehend, or simply get blocked and stop. Many struggling readers have only one tool in their fix-up toolboxes: *sound it out*. Unfortunately, decoding alone doesn't help enough at intermediate levels.

What we need to do is provide a series of tools from which to choose, modeling, reinforcing, and practicing each one. See page 70 for a flow chart showing the tools readers use to get comprehension back on track.

Comprehension Superpower: Synthesizing

Your average superhero may just have one special power, but super-readers have many. We might focus on individual strategies when it comes to instruction, but good readers rarely just use one strategy at a time. We want our student readers to be able to access the whole range of superpowers flexibly and purposefully, according to the demands of each reading situation. We want them to be aware of how their thinking shifts and their understanding evolves as they read on. We want them to be able to distill the key ideas and important messages in the text. We want them to be able to use and apply what they read to other reading and writing experiences. All this involves synthesis.

Chapter 10 offers many ideas for synthesizing understanding by writing, including a section on teaching students to summarize.

By definition, synthesis refers to the combination of components or elements to form a connected whole. Tanny McGregor (2007) uses Russian nesting dolls as a metaphor for the way our thinking evolves and expands as we read: each new piece of information or narrative detail adds another layer of meaning to our interpretation of the text. Many people equate synthesis with creating not just new understandings, but new products. Retelling, finding the main idea, and summarizing all involve synthesizing information that is read. Whenever we write in response to reading, we transform our understandings into new forms. We do the same thing when we construct mental images as we read, transforming the words on the page to pictures in our minds.

I Used to Think/But Now I Think

Students will be able to articulate their evolving thinking as they read.

Use a metaphor like the Russian stacking dolls to remind students that the super-power of synthesis involves expanding our thinking as we read. The lesson on predicting (page 59) is a good example of guiding students to confirm or adjust their thinking as they read.

1. Choose an appropriate text and plan strategic pause points at short intervals.
2. With students, read the first section of text and guide students in discussing their interpretations of what the text is about.
3. Have students read the next section of text independently, then discuss with partners how their thinking or interpretations of text have changed and why.
4. Continue this process with several more sections of text.

Must-Do Practice

Provide students with an text that has been marked with two or three pause points. Have them stop at each pause point to record their thinking on the I Used to Think… chart on page 71.

Generating Mental Images

Students will be able to intentionally generate visual images of the ideas that they read.

For many readers, visualizing is an automatic process; reading is like a movie running through their minds. Visualizing, as a strategy, involves deliberately generating a mental picture associated with the printed word. (An example of this process is the mind map on page 109.)

1. Choose an accessible text that lends itself to visual imagery and select strategic pause points.
2. Have students read the first section, then talk to partners about the image that is generated in their minds. Talk about the similarities and differences in each partner's image.
3. Continue this process with additional sections of text.

Must-Do Practice

The book Hailstones and Halibut Bones by Mary O'Neill is full of sensory images about all the colors of the rainbow and more.

Provide students with a visually rich section of text to illustrate with a labelled diagram containing pictures as well as captions. At the next group meeting, have each student share his or her visualization of the text that was read.

> **The Language of Generating Mental Images**
> - *I can just picture…*
> - *I have an image in my mind of…*
> - *It reminds me of… (sounds/ smells/ tastes/ textures)*

A Rainbow of Strategies

Students will be able to identify a range of strategies applied during reading.

This exercise can be done with any group of strategies, though I usually like to start with Connecting, Questioning, and Inferring.

1. Select a text of appropriate level and plan pause points every few paragraphs.
2. Review with students the three focus strategies and identify each with a different color of sticky notes. As they read, students track their thinking by

using appropriately colored sticky notes to tab points at which they applied any strategy.

3. After reading a section of text, students talk to a partner about what strategies they used.
4. Prepare a sheet of chart paper divided into three columns, each column headed by one of the strategies. Have students place the sticky notes they used into the appropriate columns. Talk about which strategies appeared most often and why.
5. Continue this process with two or three more sections of text.
6. Have students go back and reread the first section of text. This time, they must deliberately apply a different strategy to the passage. Follow the same process of placing the sticky notes on the chart.
7. Talk with students about what strategies they used, which were most effective, and why the strategies on a second reading differed from those on the first.

Must-Do Practice

Provide students with a text at an accessible level. Have them use the same three colors of stickies to tab the strategies they use as they read the text. (You will probably want to require a certain number of strategy tabs.) Students record their thinking directly on the sticky notes. At the next group meeting, discuss the strategies students used and which were most effective.

Strategy Bookmarks

Students will be able to respond to a variety of prompts based on strategy use.

This routine requires students to respond to a range of strategy-based prompts. You will want to teach students how to respond to each prompt before introducing this small-group lesson routine.

1. Reproduce the strategy bookmarks on page 72 and cut them apart.
2. After reading a short section of text, have each student draw a bookmark at random. Give students a few minutes to mentally prepare a response, then have each student orally share his or her response to the prompt.
3. Before moving on, invite the other students to add to or elaborate on each student's response.

Must-Do Practice

You can use the reproducible bookmarks on page 72 in a variety of ways:

- Select three or four bookmarks and have all students respond to the same prompts from a common text.
- Have students draw two or three bookmarks at random and respond from a common reading or a reading of their choice.
- Have students randomly insert three or four bookmarks into a longer text that has already been read. They complete each bookmark based on the point in the text where the bookmark is inserted.

Question Grid

	is are was were	did do does	can	will	could should would	might
Who						
What						
When/ Where						
Why						
How						
Which						

© 2014 *Struggling Readers* by Lori Jamison Rog. Pembroke Publishers. ISBN 978-1-55138-292-0

Three-Column Organizer

© 2014 *Struggling Readers* by Lori Jamison Rog. Pembroke Publishers. ISBN 978-1-55138-292-0

Inference Riddle Cards

Clue 1: People like throwing me around.
Clue 2: When somebody hits me, everyone cheers.
Clue 3: I'm battered by bats.
Clue 4: I'm either safe or out.
(Answer: a baseball)

Clue 1: You get 365 of me every year.
Clue 2: Tomorrow is another one.
Clue 3: I follow *some-* and *to-*.
Clue 4: I come before and after night.
(Answer: a day)

Clue 1: I hang out on a wall, a desk, or a computer.
Clue 2: My days are numbered.
Clue 3: I must be popular because I have so many dates.
Clue 4: I keep track of the days, weeks, and months.
(Answer: a calendar)

Clue 1: I hang out in a little hole in the wall
Clue 2: Stuff would fall down or fall apart without me.
Clue 3: People are always hammering away at me.
Clue 4: You can hang things on me.
(Answer: a nail)

Clue 1: If I'm small, I'm called a pup.
Clue 2: I like to go camping.
Clue 3: Sometimes I'm called a big top.
Clue 4: I keep the rain off you when you sleep.
(Answer: a tent)

Clue 1: I live in the dirt.
Clue 2: My future is fried.
Clue 3: I have many eyes
Clue 4: You love me with gravy.
(Answer: a potato)

Clue 1: I hate dirt.
Clue 2: I stand in the corner until it's time to clean up.
Clue 3: I get rid of crumbs, sand, and litter.
Clue 2: I'm a ride for a witch on Halloween.
(Answer: a broom)

Clue 1: I have a bed, but I never sleep.
Clue 2: I am always running, never walking.
Clue 3: I flow along, minding my own business.
Clue 4: You can cross me, but you need a bridge.
(Answer: a river)

© 2014 *Struggling Readers* by Lori Jamison Rog. Pembroke Publishers. ISBN 978-1-55138-292-0

Inference Formula Chart

I read	I know	I infer

© 2014 *Struggling Readers* by Lori Jamison Rog. Pembroke Publishers. ISBN 978-1-55138-292-0

Inferring from Pictures

What do you infer is happening here?

What do you infer happened right before the picture?

What do you infer happened right after?

© 2014 *Struggling Readers* by Lori Jamison Rog. Pembroke Publishers. ISBN 978-1-55138-292-0

Fix-Up-the-Mix-Up Flow Chart

Is the problem with a section of text?

Go back and read the section again.
Does that help?

Yes ——————————————————————————→ Go back to the text.

No
↓

Reread the section out loud to yourself.
Does that help?

Yes ——————————————————————

No
↓

Read ahead for a few sentences, then go back
to see if it helps the confusing passage makes sense.
Does that help?

Yes ——————————————————————

No
↓

Use the I Wonder strategy to try to figure out
exactly what it is that you don't understand.
Try to reduce it to a small chunk. Does that help?

Yes ——————————————————————

No
↓

Chunking the confusing part with what
comes before and what comes after.
Can you see how it all fits together? Does that help?

Yes ——————————————————————

No
↓

Try to make an inference to help you.
Think about using your background knowledge
to fill in the gaps. Does that help?

Yes ——————————————————————

No
↓

Ask for help or doing some research to
fill in missing background knowledge.

© 2014 *Struggling Readers* by Lori Jamison Rog. Pembroke Publishers. ISBN 978-1-55138-292-0

I Used to Think…

	I used to think…	but then I read…	and now I think…
Page			
Page			
Page			

© 2014 *Struggling Readers* by Lori Jamison Rog. Pembroke Publishers. ISBN 978-1-55138-292-0

Strategy Bookmarks

✂️

When I first read this section, I wondered _____,

but now I know/I think the answer is _____

_____.

✂️

When I read _____

_____,

I inferred that _____

_____.

✂️

Something I connected with in this part of the text was _____

_____

because _____

_____.

✂️

An inference (head) question about this part of the book: _____

_____ ?

A "hand" question about this part of the text: _____

_____ ?

✂️

A picture I got in my mind from this section was _____

_____.

(Sketch)

✂️

Something I inferred about the character _____

is _____.

I know this because I read _____

_____

© 2014 *Struggling Readers* by Lori Jamison Rog. Pembroke Publishers. ISBN 978-1-55138-292-0

6

Struggling Readers Need to Be Word Wise

Most of our struggling readers can decode the words they see on the page; the problem is, they don't always know what those words mean. And knowing what words mean is a pretty big deal in reading. There's a wealth of research that connects vocabulary knowledge with reading comprehension; so much so, in fact, that Andrew Biemiller (2001) calls vocabulary the "missing link" in reading instruction. Anne Cunningham and Keith Stanovich (2001) reported that a student's oral language vocabulary in Grade 1 can be a predictor of his or her reading comprehension in Grade 11!

One big problem is that our children of poverty are arriving at school with significantly fewer words than our children of affluence. By the time they are five years old, children from professional homes have heard about 45 million words, while children living in poverty have heard about 15 million. That means that before they even show up at the door of Kindergarten, there is a 30-million-word difference (Hart & Risley, 1995). Unless something is done to accelerate the vocabulary of children of poverty, that deficit will remain for their entire school careers. More than 20 years ago, Jeanne Chall and her colleagues observed children from working-class families who were competent readers in Grades 1 and 2, but fell increasingly farther behind in Grades 3 and beyond, simply because of their vocabulary limitations (Chall, 1991).

As teachers of struggling readers, we have an obligation to accelerate our students' learning of words or they will keep falling farther and farther behind, year after year. And although there is a general consensus that we must teach more words, there is no consensus on what those words should be. Isabel Beck and her colleagues (Beck, McKeown & Kucan, 2013) suggest that there are three tiers of words, depending on frequency and uniqueness:

- **Tier 1 words** constitute basic vocabulary—common nouns, verbs, and modifiers such as *girl, walk,* or *red.*
- **Tier 2 words** are more complex vocabulary for basic concepts, such as *amble, adolescent,* or *crimson.* These are often referred to as "book language" and are considered the best choices for vocabulary instruction.
- **Tier 3 words** generally are specific to one context and are often technical language, such as *chlorophyll* or *peninsula.*

Here's a quick rule-of-thumb for determining whether or not to teach a word: Choose words that your students are likely to find interesting and actually have the potential to be incorporated into students' vocabularies.

A Word-Study Program

There are plenty of effective and enlightening ways to teach vocabulary, and only one truly feckless approach. Let's start with that one. We know from years of research that assigning lists of unrelated words to be learned using the dictionary is pretty much a waste of everybody's time (Beck, McKeown & Kucan, 2013). So, we know what's ineffective. What, then, *is* effective vocabulary instruction? Michael Graves (2009) suggests that there are four components to a good word-study program:

- Providing rich and varied language experiences
- Encouraging interest in words
- Teaching specific words
- Teaching word-solving strategies

Rich Language Experiences

In an effective vocabulary classroom, we read aloud texts that contain complex vocabulary, word usage, and concepts that students would be unable to read on their own. We provide regular and frequent opportunities for sustained self-selected independent reading. We create word walls and word banks that focus on the academic vocabulary of content-area studies. We draw attention to expressive vocabulary and encourage its use in writing and talking. We raise the level of students' vocabulary by modeling interesting words in our interactions with students. All of these teacher actions provide rich experiences with language every day.

Encouraging Interest in Words

We can stimulate interest in words by playing word games, discussing jokes and riddles that involve word play, examining language origins such as Greek and Latin roots, and drawing attention to figurative language and figures of speech. Students' interest and curiosity about words are also stimulated when they learn the logic behind word origins and the stories that underlie how words came about and came to mean what they do. And it is important to realize that learning these aspects of words reveals to students that words are not only interesting—they're also fun! For example, many intermediate students enjoy *sniglets*, language phenomena defined by comedian Rich Hall (1984) as "any word that doesn't appear in the dictionary, but should." For example, *detruncus* (de trunk' us) is the embarrassing phenomenon of losing one's bathing shorts while diving into a swimming pool.

Teaching Specific Words

Usually, instruction in specific words is related to reading (text-specific vocabulary) and content-area studies (academic vocabulary). Andrew Biemiller (2001) found that something as simple as defining new words as you read aloud can make a difference to students' vocabularies. Generally speaking, however, students need many exposures to new words in different contexts in order to incorporate them into their working vocabularies, to make a word their own. They need to understand how new words connect to the words they know and how

To preteach or not to preteach? Is the word essential to understanding of the passage? Are there enough contextual supports for the reader to figure it out on his/her own?

these words change in different situations. If we want our students to make a new vocabulary word their own, the students must have reasons and opportunities to actually use the word.

In the past, we've assumed that preteaching vocabulary is essential to prepare students for reading a piece of text. In truth, most readers can't hold more than a couple of new words in their heads as they try to navigate an unfamiliar text. Vocabulary instruction is much more effective in the context of reading.

Sometimes we will need to teach some key vocabulary before reading a passage. If a word is essential to understanding the passage and your readers are unlikely to be able to figure it out on their own, take a few minutes to preteach it. But limit the preteaching to two or three words. Then consider the remaining vocabulary words. How important is it for students to make these words their own? If a word has little application outside the specific reading, then a brief review will suffice; if it's a word students might be able to apply in their academic or out-of-school lives, use processes like MOVES (page 75) and/or Vocabulary Squares (page 76).

Word-Solving Strategies

The final component of Graves's word-study curriculum is providing students with tools for figuring out unfamiliar words as they read. One of the reasons many struggling readers are dysfluent and stumble in their comprehension is that they don't recognize enough words instantly. It's important that readers be able to read automatically most words they encounter and be able to decipher the remaining words with relative ease, using a range of word-solving strategies.

Many of our struggling readers lack flexibility in word-solving. Often their word-solving strategies are limited to *sound it out* or *skip it*, neither of which helps much with repairing comprehension. Decoding tells us only how to pronounce the word, not what it means. Many struggling readers have trouble inferring word meanings from context clues alone, but pairing context clues with breaking the word into chunks of meaning (i.e., root words and affixes) can be the most effective combination in the word-solving toolkit (Nagy, Anderson, & Herman, 1987). See page 84 for a flow chart of word-solving strategies.

Lesson Routines for Vocabulary and World-Solving

Vocabulary MOVES

Students will be able to learn and recall new vocabulary by experiencing a variety of learning modes.

The more exposures we have to a word, the more likely we are to remember and learn it. Learning is further reinforced when those exposures are in different contexts and modes.

The MOVES protocol starts with revisiting the focus word in context and follows five steps to expose the word to the students in different ways or contexts:

1. **Meaning:** Provide a learner-friendly definition of the word.
2. **Other Context:** Offer an alternative example or context for the word, different from the one in the original reading.
3. **Visual:** Help students take a visual picture of the word to help them remember it in future.

Vocabulary MOVES
Meaning
Other Context
Visual
External Experience
Slip into conversation

4. External Experience: Help students create an engaging external experience for the word; experiences might include a gesture, a mental picture, a mnemonic gesture, an artifact, or a game.

5. Slip into Conversation: Try to create conditions for the focus word(s) to come up. Keep a checklist of every time a word is used during the day. (If you have two or three focus words, see which one is used most often, or "wins.") As an "exit slip" for dismissal, ask students to give a sentence using one of the words.

Sample of MOVES at Work

In the story *Charlotte's Web*, Charlotte is described as having a big *vocabulary*.
Meaning: "*Vocabulary* means a set of words in the language."
Other Context: "When you're learning a new language, like French, you need to build your *vocabulary*. There is also a certain special *vocabulary* associated with computers, including words such as *hyperlink* or *gigabyte*. Even in English, when someone uses a lot of interesting words, we say he or she has a big *vocabulary*."
Visual: "We can chunk the word *vocabulary* into five syllables. Let's chunk it and visualize a wave under each of the syllables."
External Experience: "I'll say some words in French and I'd like you to give a thumbs-up for every word that is in your French vocabulary: Give a thumbs-up if *bonjour* is part of French vocabulary. Give a thumbs-up if the word *spaghetti* is part of French vocabulary." Note that the focus word *vocabulary* is repeated each time.
Slip into Conversation: "Let's keep track of how often we hear any of us use the word *vocabulary* today."

Must-Do Practice

Invite students to try to use the focus word(s) as often as you can during the day. Alternatively, have students create Vocabulary Squares (described in the next lesson) for one or more of the words.

Vocabulary Squares

Students will be able to assimilate vocabulary words by applying context, meaning, a personal connection, and a visual reminder.

The Vocabulary Square is a terrific tool for reinforcing words learned in reading or content areas. An adaptation of the Frayer Model (Frayer, Frederick & Klausmeier, 1969), the Vocabulary Square is intended to provide a visual representation of the attributes and non-attributes of concept words. In this design, visual images and personal connections are incorporated to help students recall and retain a focus word.

1. Demonstrate how to create a Vocabulary Square by reproducing the one on page 85 or by simply folding a piece of paper in four. (Fold a triangle up at the point where two folded sides of the paper meet and it will form a diamond in the centre when unfolded.)
2. Complete the graphic organizer as follows:
   • Centre Diamond: Write the focus word.
   • Top Left Box: Copy the phrase or sentence in which the word is found.
   • Top Right Box: Write a definition of the word, preferably in your own words rather than copied from a dictionary.
   • Bottom Right Box: Draw a picture, symbol, or icon for a visual reminder of what the word means.
   • Bottom Left Box: Note a personal connection that will help you remember the word.

Have students complete a vocabulary square on one or more of the focus words presented in class. Provide opportunities for students to share their vocabulary squares with partners on a subsequent group meeting.

Storm and Sort

Students will be able to expand their vocabularies by sorting and categorizing familiar and unfamiliar words.

Word sorting is a valuable instructional routine in which words are learned by grouping them into categories. This routine is particularly useful for struggling readers, because it requires them to compare, contrast, and look for patterns as they build vocabulary knowledge. We can't possibly teach students every word they will need to know, but we can teach broad categories of words into which new words will be integrated.

Storm and Sort is a teacher-guided activity that is possible to do with large groups, but it works best in small groups.

Each stage of this routine has an important role: harvesting interesting words from a reading passage or content-area study; analyzing similarities and differences among words; identifying and labeling groups; and extending vocabulary by adding words to the groups.

> **Storm and Sort Process**
> 1. Brainstorm or gather words.
> 2. Sort into groups or categories.
> 3. Give a name to each category.
> 4. Extend and enrich by adding new words to each group.

1. Start by brainstorming words related to a theme, or selecting a collection of words from a reading passage or from a content-area study. My preference for struggling readers is to create individual word cards for students to manipulate as they sort the words into categories.
2. To introduce the routine, work collaboratively as a group to sort these words into categories. Sometimes I will suggest the categories; often I do not. There are many ways to sort a set of words and, if the words are worth remembering, it's probably worth revisiting the list several times to sort it in different ways. Words can be sorted by syllables, part of speech, or letter features, for example; however, if the purpose of the activity is to build vocabulary, then I think it's essential to sort by semantic features—in other words, by meaning. Rules for sorting include the following:
   - There must be at least two groups; there can be as many as you need.
   - There must be at least two words in a group.
   - Some words might fit into more than one group.
   - Every word must be put in a group.
3. After the words have been sorted, students should give a name or label to each category.
4. To extend the experience, ask students to try to add words of their own to each category.

Must-Do Practice

This routine might be an end in itself, or you can choose to have students work further with the words; for example, by making vocabulary flap books. See page 52 for instructions on how to make a flap book. Once the strips have been cut, write one vocabulary word on each outside tab. Under the flap, students can write a definition, use the word in a sentence, and/or draw an illustration for each word.

Vocabulary Highlights

Students will be able to identify challenging words in connected text.

It's important that students be able to identify words that cause them to stumble, then apply a range of strategies to solving those words. In fact, vocabulary instruction is much more effective when it occurs in the context of reading than if it is done before the reading begins.

1. Have students use highlighting tape to select two or three challenging vocabulary words in the text. It's been my experience that struggling readers either don't know or are reluctant to admit that they have trouble with any words. So I find it more efficient to ask them to highlight two or three words "that *someone else* might have trouble with."
2. Make a list of words chosen by the students and use these for instruction. You might choose to engage students in some sorting activities, Vocabulary Squares, or word games using the selected words.

Must-Do Practice

Have students work in pairs to extend the list of focus words with synonyms, antonyms, words from the same origin or root-word family, etc. Invite them to add two or three related words to each word in the list. At the next small-group session, have students share their words and explain how they are related to the focus words.

Context Clues

Students will be able to use context clues in the text to define an unfamiliar word.

Context clues are words in the text that define or help us understand a particular vocabulary word. Context clues are more likely to be found in nonfiction text than in fiction. There are four main types of context clues, each with its own unique set of signal words that indicate that a clue is present.

Context Clues and Signal Words

Type of Context Clue	What It Does	Possible Signal Words
Definition	Gives the meaning directly	• which means • is defined as
Restatement or Synonym	Repeats the word in a different way or using other words that mean the same thing	• in other words • or • which is the same as
Contrast or Antonym	Tells the opposite meaning	• as opposed to • alternatively • in contrast to
Example	Gives examples of the word or concept	• such as • for example • like

1. Display four multiple-choice items for students to read; for example:

   Elliptical shapes are oval with rounded sides.
     a) shaped like an egg
     b) shaped like an ice cube
     c) shaped like a full moon

   Aquatic animals are creatures that live in the ocean.
     a) from the desert
     b) from the water
     c) from the arctic
     d) from the mountains

   Nutritious foods help our bodies grow, but too many unhealthy foods may make us sick.
     a) tasty
     b) sickly
     c) healthy

   Our class went to the museum and we saw many *artifacts*, such as fossils, dinosaur bones, and petrified wood.
     a) ideas
     b) objects
     c) pictures

2. For each italicized word, have students select the correct definition, then identify the context clues that support the meaning of the word.
3. Talk about what type of clue each represents. You might want to show students the Context Clues and Signal Words chart on page 78, or guide students in constructing their own anchor chart.

Must-Do Practice

Reproduce Context Clues: Reading Around the Word on page 86 and have the students work individually or in pairs to select the correct meaning and identify the context clues for each word. This type of exercise gives students practice in responding to multiple-choice items and justifying choices, which will help them tackle large-scale assessments.

Chunking Words

Most of the words that cause problems for our struggling readers have three or more syllables. Struggling readers are sometimes intimidated simply by looking at these long words! Yet multi-syllabic words can be very easy to read if we chunk them into syllables.

The problem is that syllable chunking doesn't always help with the meanings of words. But breaking words into morphological chunks, or chunks of meaning—such as prefixes, suffixes, and roots—can help with both the pronunciation and the meaning of words. Teaching students about the various affixes and what they mean is important, but the most important word part is the root. It's easy to find the roots in words like *running* or *unhappy* or *equipment,* as they are whole English words. But sometimes the root words are not so evident, in words such as *repeat* or *spectator.*

Studying words from other languages can be interesting to readers of all ages, though struggling readers will need plenty of teacher support and scaffolding.

An Internet search of "context clues practice" will provide many more exercises of this nature.

Students will be able to solve unfamiliar words by looking for root words.

Technically speaking, *base* words are complete English words while *root* words are derivatives from other languages. For the purposes of this book, we'll refer to them all as *root words.*

Most of the unfamiliar roots in English come from Latin or Greek; see page 87 for a list of common roots. With luck, you'll find that your students will become quite fascinated with the world of words.

1. Give students three fairly common words derived from the same root: for example, the verbs *subtract, extract*, and *attract*. See Roots and Derivatives chart below.
2. Have students work in teams to identify the root and define it, based on their understanding of the focus words. Talk about what aspects of meaning the three words have in common: for example, "*Subtract* means to take away and *extract* means to pull out, like a tooth. But *attract* means to pull toward. Maybe they all have to do with pulling, either toward or away from."
3. Provide an unfamiliar word with the same root (for example, *detract*) and have students apply what they know of the root (and affix) to try to define the word: for example, "*De-* means 'away from' or 'opposite'. So I think *detract* must mean to pull away from."
4. Have students compare their definition with a dictionary definition: The dictionary says that "detract" means to take away the value of something.
5. Invite students to use their own background knowledge, print and online dictionaries, and other resources to generate additional words with the same root: for example, other words derived from the root *tract* include *contract, distract*, or *abstract*.

Must-Do Practice

Have students work in pairs through the process using the examples below: explaining the root; defining the new word; and coming up with additional words. Of course, dictionary use is encouraged!

Sample Roots and Derivatives

Root	Anchor Words	New Word
Latin: *pend*, to hang	pendulum, pendant, depend	append
Latin: *tract*, to pull or drag	subtract, extract, attract	detract
Latin: *dict*, to say	dictate, dictionary, predict	contradict
Latin: *port*, to carry	transport, import, support	deportment
Latin: *scrip*, writing	description, prescription, scripture	transcription
Latin: *videre*, to see	vision, visit, revise	supervise
Greek: *phone*, sound, voice	telephone, microphone, megaphone	cacophony
Greek: *ped* or *pod*, feet	tripod, podium, podiatrist	pedometer
Greek: *poli*, city	police, political, metropolitan	megalopolis

Powerful Prefixes and Super Suffixes

Students will be able to understand and use affixes for solving unfamiliar words.

Prefixes and suffixes, known collectively as *affixes,* are added to the beginning or end of a root word to change the meaning or part of speech (or both).

Prefixes are easier than suffixes. They never change the spelling or the part of speech of the root word or part of speech. Most of them are fairly specific in meaning; in fact, of the 20 common prefixes listed on page 90, six of them change a word to mean "not" or the opposite.

Suffixes are a little more complex. *Inflectional suffixes* like *–ed* and *-ing* generally don't change the meaning of a word; they adjust a word grammatically to make it fit the sentence, such as making the word plural or putting it in the past tense. *Derivational suffixes* are tricky, because they often change the part of speech *and* may also change the meaning of a word: add *-er* to *teach* and you get *teacher,* a noun for someone who teaches; add *-ly* to the adjective *loud* and you get *loudly,* an adverb that tells how something is said or done. There are hundreds of derivational suffixes. A list of some common suffixes may be found on page 89.

Your most capable readers probably know most of the common prefixes and suffixes, and you can probably review them on an as-needed basis. But your struggling readers might benefit from a more methodical introduction to these important morphological chunks. The Nifty Thrifty Fifty is a list of words compiled by Patricia Cunningham and Dorothy Hall (1998) to represent the most frequently appearing prefixes, suffixes, roots, and spelling changes in our language. Cunningham and Hall suggest teaching a handful of these words each month, spending time reading, writing, and analyzing these words before moving on to another set.

Fifty Words for Teaching Common Prefixes, Suffixes, and Roots
(Adapted from Cunningham & Hall, 1998)

antifreeze	employee	invasion	semifinal
beautiful	encouragement	irresponsible	signature
classify	expensive	midnight	submarine
communities	forecast	misunderstand	supermarkets
community	forgotten	musician	swimming
composer	governor	nonliving	transportation
continuous	happiness	overpower	underweight
conversation	hopeless	performance	unfinished
deodorize	illegal	prehistoric	unfriendly
different	impossible	prettier	unpleasant
discovery	impression	rearrange	valuable
dishonest	independence	replacement	
electricity	international	richest	

---

1. Create an enlarged anchor chart like the Chunking Chart on page 82.
2. Choose three words from the list above, such as *composer, unfriendly,* and *impossible.* Work with students to identify the prefixes, suffixes, and roots.
3. Discuss how the prefixes and suffixes change the meaning, part of speech, and spelling of each word.
4. Brainstorm additional words associated with each prefix, suffix, and root.

You might want to check out Patricia Cunningham and Dorothy Hall's book *Month by Month Phonics for the Upper Grades*, or conduct an Internet search to find a range of ways that teachers have used the Nifty Thrifty Fifty in teaching morphological chunks.

Sample Chunking Anchor Chart

NTF Word	Root	Prefix	Suffix	Spelling Change	Other Words
composer	compose – to write or create a work of art		-er – someone who is or does	Drop the final e	teacher farmer
unfriendly	friend – someone you like or feel affection for	un- –not	-ly – like, similar to		unhappily unkind saintly
impossible	possible – capable of happening	im- – not			imperfect immovable

Must-Do Practice

Create two dice: one with six familiar prefixes and suffixes that have already been studied, and one with six roots that are unfamiliar. Have students work in pairs to take turns rolling the dice and putting together the root and affix rolled to see if they create actual words or nonsense words. You can make it a competition by allocating one point for each real word rolled and a bonus point if the student can define the word.

Outside the Word/Inside the Word

Students will be able to integrate context clues and morphological chunks for solving unfamiliar words.

Neither inferring from surrounding text nor breaking down a word into meaningful chunks alone are failsafe decoding tools. However, in combination they are probably the most effective word-solving strategy we have, especially for struggling readers (Biemiller, 2001). The first thing struggling readers need to do is recognize when they encounter a word they don't know; the next thing is to apply strategies for solving that word. One effective process for solving unfamiliar words is to read *outside the word* to see if there are context clues nearby, then read *inside the word* to see if there are root or affixes that help confirm the meaning.

For example, look at this sentence: *I lost my keys, but luckily I had a duplicate set so I could get into my house.* We know from *duo* and *double* that the prefix *du-* probably means *two*. And the suffix *-ate* means *to make*, as in *abbreviate* or *educate*. From the context of the sentence, the meaning of *duplicate* can be inferred as *making a copy* or *creating two* keys.

1. Provide students with a set of sentences, for example:

   We weren't sure if the berries were *edible*, so we decided not to eat them.
   The campers surrounded the campfire in a *semicircular* formation.
   I couldn't get my hair cut because my hairdresser was *unavailable*.

2. Work with students to identify the prefixes, suffixes, and roots of each italicized word.
3. Invite students to try to define the words based on the morphological structure.

4. Go back into the sentences to confirm, correct, or expand on the definitions.
5. Tell students that sometimes context around the word will give stronger clues to the meaning of a word and sometimes chunks of the word itself will give better clues, but combining both what's "inside the word" and what's "outside the word" will be the most reliable.
6. If students need more guided practice using the inside and outside of the word, use some of the sentences on page 88.

Must-Do Practice

Choose examples from the Inside the Word/Outside the Word list on page 88 or create examples of your own to provide practice in using morphology and context clues to figure out the meanings of unfamiliar words.

Word Explosions

Students will be able to expand words by adding prefixes and suffixes.

We need our struggling readers to see that if they know one root word, they can expand it to tens and sometimes hundreds of words. Word explosions are maps of roots, derivatives, and various forms of those derivatives created by adding prefixes and suffixes; see sample below.

1. Start by modeling and collaborating with students how word explosions work.
2. In the centre of the page, write the root and its meaning.
3. Around the word, record four to six words derived from that root, along with their meanings.
4. Around each of those words, create as many forms of the word as possible by adding prefixes and suffixes.
5. Give students large sheets of chart paper and plenty of colored markers. Turn them loose in small groups to create their own word-explosion posters.

Must-Do Practice

Have students work in pairs to select a word and create a word explosion. Some words you might use are *mechanic, elect, create, explore, happy.*

Sample Word Explosion

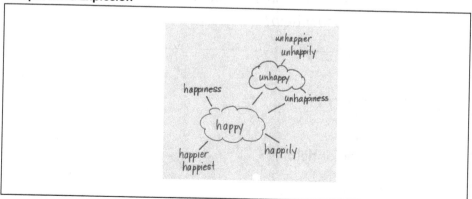

Word-Solving Flow Chart

Having trouble with a word?

➔ Read on to see if you can get the gist of the passage without knowing that word. Does that help?

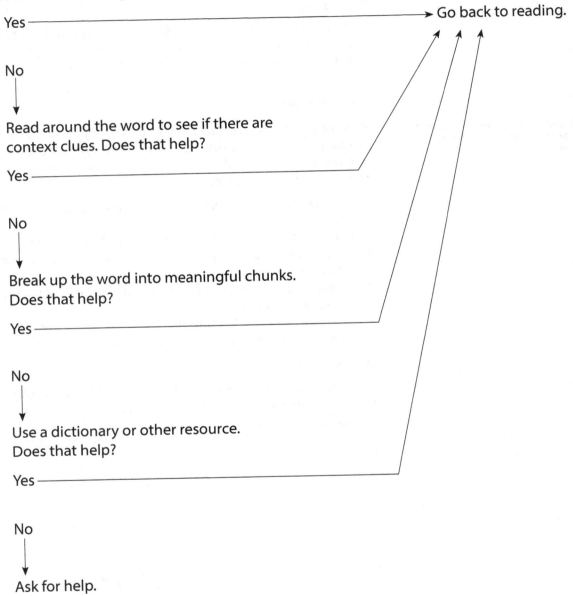

Yes ——————————————————————→ Go back to reading.

No
↓

Read around the word to see if there are context clues. Does that help?

Yes ——————

No
↓

Break up the word into meaningful chunks. Does that help?

Yes ——————

No
↓

Use a dictionary or other resource. Does that help?

Yes ——————

No
↓

Ask for help.

© 2014 *Struggling Readers* by Lori Jamison Rog. Pembroke Publishers. ISBN 978-1-55138-292-0

Vocabulary Square

Context	Definition

Focus Word

Personal Connection	Visual

© 2014 *Struggling Readers* by Lori Jamison Rog. Pembroke Publishers. ISBN 978-1-55138-292-0

Context Clues: Reading Around the Word

Read around each key word in bold print to figure out what it means. Then use a highlighting pen to mark the words that give clues to the meaning of each key word. If there are signal words, highlight them in a different color.

1. Our class went to the museum and we saw many **artifacts**, such as fossils, dinosaur bones, and petrified wood.
    - a) ideas
    - b) objects
    - c) pictures

2. The fall **foliage** is wonderful to see, with its blends of red, orange, and gold.
    - a) leaves
    - b) animals
    - c) weather

3. A **sleuth**, or detective, needs to pay attention to many clues.
    - a) singer
    - b) dentist
    - c) teacher
    - d) police officer

4. The kitten was so **fascinated** with the piece of foil that she played with it for hours.
    - a) unhappy
    - b) frustrated
    - c) interested

5. It was so hot in the attic that we had to **ventilate** it using a fan.
    - a) air it out
    - b) dry it out
    - c) dust it off

6. Dark clouds warned of the **impending** storm and we rushed to look for shelter before the rain began.
    - a) snow
    - b) deadly
    - c) coming

7. Although some people are **loquacious**, others hardly talk at all.
    - a) see a lot
    - b) talk a lot
    - c) know a lot
    - d) listen a lot

8. The lawyer's argument was **fallacious**, or misleading.
    - a) honest
    - b) not true
    - c) full of big words

9. **Celestial** bodies, such as planets and moons, orbit around the sun.
    - a) found in outer space
    - b) found in horoscopes
    - c) found in science books

10. The **osprey**, a large bird that eats mostly fish, is found all over the world.
    - a) a water bird
    - b) a jungle bird
    - c) a desert bird

11. At first the patient seemed to be doing well, but later his condition began to **deteriorate**.
    - a) get better
    - b) get worse
    - c) stay the same

12. We thought my mother would be **distraught** when she crashed the car but surprisingly she was quite calm.
    - a) upset
    - b) happy
    - c) injured

© 2014 *Struggling Readers* by Lori Jamison Rog. Pembroke Publishers. ISBN 978-1-55138-292-0

Common Latin and Greek Roots

Latin Root	Basic Meaning	Example Words
-dict-	to say	contradict, dictate, diction, edict, predict
-duc-	to lead, bring, take	deduce, produce, reduce
-gress-	to walk	digress, progress, transgress
-ject-	to throw	eject, inject, interject, project, reject, subject
-pel-	to drive	compel, dispel, impel, repel
-pend-	to hang	append, depend, impend, pendant, pendulum
-port-	to carry	comport, deport, export, import, report, support
-scrib-, -script-	to write	describe, description, prescribe, prescription, subscribe, subscription, transcribe, transcription
-tract-	to pull, drag, draw	attract, contract, detract, extract, protract, retract, traction
-vert-	to turn	convert, divert, invert, revert

Greek Root	Basic Meaning	Example Words
-anthrop-	human	misanthrope, philanthropy, anthropomorphic
-chron-	time	anachronism, chronic, chronicle, synchronize, chronometer
-dem-	people	democracy, demography, demagogue, endemic, pandemic
-morph-	form	amorphous, metamorphic, morphology
-path-	feeling, suffering	empathy, sympathy, apathy, apathetic, psychopathic
-pedo-, -ped-	child, children	pediatrician, pedagogue
-philo-, -phil-	having a strong affinity or love for	philanthropy, philharmonic, philosophy
-phon-	sound	polyphonic, cacophony, phonetics

© 2014 *Struggling Readers* by Lori Jamison Rog. Pembroke Publishers. ISBN 978-1-55138-292-0

Outside the Word/Inside the Word

Look at the cues outside and inside each of the underlined key words to figure out what the word means. Take a guess at what the words mean, then check your meanings with a dictionary.

Sentence	Your Definition	Dictionary Definition
The birds were <u>unmistakably</u> male peacocks because of their bright tail feathers.		
The <u>reversible</u> blanket was gray on one side and red on the other.		
Jada helped Mom with the dinner <u>preparations</u> by setting the table.		
We were laughing <u>uncontrollably</u> and just couldn't stop.		
<u>Refillable</u> bottles are better for the environment than <u>disposable</u> bottles.		
She sat <u>uncomfortably</u> on the hard wooden bench through the long church service.		
Dad <u>miscalculated</u> the distance to the park and he ran out of gas.		
I was too warm so I zipped the <u>removable</u> hood off my jacket.		
Be sure to bring a bottle of water on the hike so you don't become <u>dehydrated</u>.		
His handwriting was so messy that his story was <u>unreadable</u>.		

© 2014 *Struggling Readers* by Lori Jamison Rog. Pembroke Publishers. ISBN 978-1-55138-292-0

Common Suffixes

Suffix	Example Words	What It Means	How It Changes the Root Word
-able, -ible	comfortable edible ("eatable")	can be done, capable of being	Changes a noun to an adjective
-al	denial	act or process of	Changes a verb to a noun
-al	accidental	pertaining to, having characteristics of	Changes a noun to an adjective
-en	woolen, wooden	made of	Changes a noun to an adjective
-er, -or	teacher dictator	someone who does	Changes a verb to a noun
-er, -est	smarter, smartest	more, most	Makes the adjective comparative
-ful	wonderful, careful	full of	Changes a noun to an adjective
-ian	musician electrician	someone who does	Turns a concept or thing into a person
-ion, -tion, -sion (-ation, -ition)	attraction exploration persuasion	an act or process	Makes a verb into a noun
-ize (-ise)	terrorize	to do, enact, cause	Makes a noun into a verb
-ity, -ty	electricity infinity	state or quality of	Changes an adjective to a noun
-ive, (-ative, -itive)	creative	having the nature of	Changes a verb to an adjective
-less	hopeless	without	Changes a noun to an adjective
-ly	happily	characteristic of	Changes an adjective to an adverb
-ment	retirement excitement	process or event	Changes a verb to a noun
-ness	kindness	state or condition of	Changes an adjective to a noun
-ous (-eous, -ious)	joyous gracious beauteous	having the qualities of	Changes a noun to an adjective
-y	bouncy	characterized by	Changes a verb or noun to an adjective

© 2014 *Struggling Readers* by Lori Jamison Rog. Pembroke Publishers. ISBN 978-1-55138-292-0

Common Prefixes

Prefix	Example Words	How It Changes the Root Word
anti-	antibiotic	Makes it mean against or in opposition to
de-	defrost declutter	Makes the opposite, removes, reduces
dis-	disagree disappoint	Makes it mean the opposite
en-, em-	entangle embitter	To cause it to be
fore-	foreshadow forecast	Before, ahead of time
in-, im-, il-, ir-	injustice impossible illegitimate irresponsible	Makes it mean the opposite
mis-	misfire, misunderstand	To do it incorrectly
non-	nonsensical	Makes it mean the opposite
over-	overlook, overhang	To do it from above
pre-	prefix	To do it before
re-	redecorate, retell	To do it again
semi-	semifinal, semicircle	Half or part of it
sub-	submarine, subterranean	Under or below
super-	supervisor, superstar	To be above, higher in status or position
trans-	transport	To do it across
un-	unkind	Makes it mean the opposite
under-	underwear	To do it under

© 2014 *Struggling Readers* by Lori Jamison Rog. Pembroke Publishers. ISBN 978-1-55138-292-0

7

Struggling Readers Need to Build Fluency

I was a pretty good reader in Grade 3. I looked forward each day to reading time, when I could dazzle my classmates with dramatic renditions of the adventures of Dick, Jane, and Sally. Unfortunately, reading time meant that Davey, sitting behind me, also had to read, in spite of his best efforts to avoid it. Day after day, the whole class sat and squirmed while Davey read aloud, word by painful word. While the event was uncomfortable for the rest of us, it was torture for Davey. And it didn't make any of us better readers.

When I became a teacher, I resolved to eliminate the painful and pedagogically unsound practice of having all students take turns reading aloud, a practice known as round-robin reading. But without an alternative, I essentially eliminated oral reading altogether. And the metaphorical baby I threw out with this bathwater was development of reading fluency. As long as my students could read the words, I reasoned, why did it matter whether they could read those words smoothly and automatically?

Fluency Matters

I've since learned that fluency *does* matter. Research tells us that the ability to read quickly, accurately, and with appropriate intonation and phrasing is closely linked to overall comprehension (National Reading Panel, 2000). In essence, fluency provides a bridge between reading the words and understanding the text. We know that effective readers, even at early levels, read in five- to seven-word phrases rather than word-by-word (Allington, 2001). Dysfluent readers, on the other hand, devote so much effort and energy to reading individual words, they have little working memory left to devote to overall comprehension and interpretation.

When readers read slowly, they read less. Because it takes them longer to read a text, they experience less reading volume than those who are faster readers. We know that there's a link between how *much* you read and how *well* you read. The Report of the National Reading Panel (2000) asserts that "there is ample evidence that one of the major differences between poor and good readers is the difference in the quantity of total time they spend reading" (NRP: 3–10).

There are other repercussions to slow reading, according to Tim Rasinski (2000). Picture, for example, a Grade 6 classroom in which the students are assigned a chapter to read in their science textbooks. The slow reader notices that everyone around has completed the reading when he/she is only halfway through. Does this student keep plodding along, hoping that no one will notice that he/she is the last one done? More likely, the student skims through the last half of the chapter, or skips it all together. As a result, he/she isn't exposed to the same information as the others, missing not only the content of that particular science class, but valuable background knowledge to help with further reading.

Why do some readers read slowly and hesitantly? Some teachers believe that dysfluent reading is caused by weak decoding skills. Yet studies of struggling older readers indicate that they often have better vocabularies and more phonics knowledge than younger fluent readers (Allington, 2001). Dysfluent reading is not a likely result of a lack of phonics, but in many cases, comes from an *over-reliance* on phonics. Many dysfluent readers tend to sound out words, letter by letter. They might read nonsense words without stopping to self-correct. Or if something doesn't make sense to them, they often simply stop and wait for help rather than trying other strategies.

That's not to say that good readers don't need to decode unfamiliar words. Good readers also use phonics, but as only one tool in a repertoire of strategies. Their decoding tends to be smooth and automatic, seeking out chunks and patterns in words rather than sounding words out letter by letter. Because decoding is less laborious, fluent readers have enough cognitive resources available to connect, interpret, and synthesize as they read. This enables these readers to monitor their own comprehension as they read, rereading and cross-checking if something doesn't make sense.

The Fluency Gap

Fluent readers are more likely to…	Dysfluent readers are more likely to…
…read with appropriate pacing and phrasing.	…read hesitantly, word by word.
…decode words by patterns and chunks.	… sound out words letter by letter.
…make use of punctuation for meaning and phrasing.	…ignore punctuation and pause at inappropriate times.
…flexibly use a variety of word-solving strategies.	…use phonics as the dominant (if not exclusive) cueing strategy.
…be allowed to make mistakes without interruption.	…be interrupted whenever they make a miscue.
…monitor their own comprehension.	…rely on the teacher to prompt.
…go back and reread and cross-check if the reading doesn't make sense.	…read on whether or not the reading makes sense.

Dick Allington (2001) suggests that, in many cases, dysfluent reading might be a conditioned behavior, unwittingly perpetuated by teachers. He reports that teachers are quicker to interrupt struggling readers when they make a miscue. Struggling readers are more often stopped and told to sound it out before they even have a chance to notice their own errors. As a result, these readers become even more hesitant about their own reading, never knowing when they're going to be corrected. They also learn to rely on the teacher to tell them when they've made a mistake rather than learning to monitor their own reading.

The good news about dysfluency is that it is not a permanent affliction. Fluency can be taught and practiced in a variety of effective and engaging ways.

What Can Teachers Do?

Although most of the reading our students in Grades 3 to 9 will do is silent, the only way to build, sustain, and assess reading fluency is by having students read aloud. We need to provide authentic opportunities for oral reading, always ensuring that readers have a chance to preread and practice before reading publicly. And we need to make sure that the texts students read are within their ability.

1. Ensure that materials are at appropriate reading levels

We all struggle with reading when the text is too difficult for us. What if you or I had to read a complicated technical treatise on current developments in brain surgery? We'd probably be missing essential background knowledge and would struggle with much of the vocabulary. Quite likely, we would hesitate, miscue, go back and reread, and sometimes even fake it, just as our students do. If we want our students to read with fluency, we need to ensure that the texts they read aren't beyond their capabilities.

2. Never require students to read publicly without practicing first

Sharing reading aloud needn't be an event; we can build oral reading into instruction by asking a student, for example, to "read the paragraph that describes the setting of the story" or "read the section that tells how the emperor penguin cares for his eggs" or "share the paragraph/page that you found most interesting." Not only is this a natural way to invite oral reading, it also ensures that students will have an opportunity to read and rehearse ahead of time.

3. Help students build automaticity in word reading

Ideas for helping students develop independent word-solving strategies can be found in Chapter 6.

We need to help students build a repertoire of words that they can read automatically. We must teach students to smoothly and efficiently integrate a variety of word-solving strategies for the words they don't immediately recognize. Finally, we have to train ourselves to give our students the opportunity to recognize and correct their own miscues. Even waiting for three to five seconds before intervening in a student's reading will help him/her develop essential self-monitoring strategies.

4. Avoid round-robin reading

It's pretty obvious that for learners like Davey, this practice can kill both their skill and will as readers. But the other issue is that, in round-robin reading, there simply isn't much reading going on. What are the students who aren't on the spot doing? They're probably reading ahead, counting paragraphs, or merely daydreaming. Even those who want to read along are likely to have trouble, because one person's silent reading rate rarely matches another person's oral reading rate. Following the print while someone else reads can actually interfere with one's own fluency. As for the individual who's doing the reading, he or she is likely to be focusing on sounding good rather than attending to what the text is all about. All the things we teach readers to do—make connections, pause and reflect, engage in self-talk, go back and reread—are lost in the process.

Oral Reading Practices that Support Fluency

Modeling with Read-Alouds

The simplest and best way for students to hear what fluent readers do is for teachers to model with engaging read-alouds. This is why it's important for teachers to preview and even practice reading a book before reading it to students, just to ensure that they are providing the best possible model. Even most nonfiction text today is full of voice and should be read with passion and enthusiasm. Sometimes reading aloud even the first section of a passage before students read the rest independently can set a tone and style for students to emulate.

Books on tape can provide another model of effective reading, especially those read by professional actors. Check out the Book Pals program from the Screen Actors' Guild, in which prominent actors read popular children's books. Do remember, though, that a taped reading doesn't allow for the pauses to reflect and question that a teacher read-aloud can.

Shared Reading

The shared book experience is traditionally characterized by the use of common text that is visible to a large group of students, such as a Big Book, a chart, or onscreen print. The text is meant to be revisited several times, with the teacher modeling first and then gradually fading out as the students take over the reading.

Some people have adapted the shared-reading process for upper-grade students by having students follow along from their own text while the teacher, an audio book reader, or another student reads. The problem with this practice is that students may hear a model of fluent reading, but they are not reading much themselves. Struggling readers, in particular, simply can't keep up with the reading speed of a fluent reader. The chart below summarizes classic research by Jan Hasbrouck and Gerald Tindal (2006). These figures represent the top (90th percentile), average (50th percentile), and lowest (10th percentile) readers at the end of the grade level. According to this data, a struggling eighth-grader is likely to be reading more slowly than an average third-grader.

Oral Reading Fluency: Average Correct Words/Minute at the End of the Year

Percentile	Grade 3	Grade 4	Grade 5	Grade 6	Grade 7	Grade 8
90th	162	180	194	204	202	199
50th	107	123	139	150	150	151
10th	48	72	83	93	98	97

A more traditional shared reading process (see box on page 95) can be very effective for replacing choppy, word-by-word reading with smooth, expressive phrases. Start by choosing an interesting and engaging text—rhythmical texts, such as poems and song lyrics, are ideal choices for fluency building. The teacher reads the text first, providing a fluent model. Gradually, the students join in on subsequent readings, with the teacher eventually fading out his/her voice out and leaving the students to read chorally and individually. It is this repeated reading that has been shown to best support fluency (Therrien & Kubina, 2006).

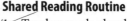

> **Shared Reading Routine**
> 1. Teacher reads aloud with fluency and expression.
> 2. Teacher reads line by line and students echo.
> 3. Teacher and students read chorally, with teacher fading out as students take over.
> 4. Students read individually in unison without teacher support.

Choral Reading

Choral reading involves a group reading in unison or chorus. This practice builds fluency because struggling readers are pulled along in the reading with more fluent readers. Choral reading is an integral part of the shared reading experience and there are many variations to maintain interest over several repeated readings, such as the following:

- Have students read in different voices (e.g., cowboy voice, opera voice, squeaky voice, growly voice, etc.).
- Have students take turns reading one line at a time.
- Assign different parts of the piece to be read by different students. Give them an opportunity to prepare how they will read their sections.
- Flash-mob reading: One person starts and gradually others join in until the entire group is reading. Then try the opposite—going from the whole group to a single reader.

The following poems by Paul Fleishman are ideal for choral reading, as they involve responses and multiple voices: *Big Talk: Poems for Four Voices* **(Candlewick, 2000);** *Joyful Noises: Poems for Two Voices* **(HarperTrophy, 1992);** *I am Phoenix: Poems for Two Voices* **(HarperTrophy, 1989)**

Paired Reading

According to the report of the National Reading Panel (2000), guided repeated oral reading is the most effective procedure for developing reading fluency. This process involves giving students an opportunity to read a passage aloud, to receive feedback on their reading, then to reread the passage again and again until they have reached a desired level of fluency with that particular text.

When one partner is a more capable reader than the other, such as in the case of a tutor, parent, or even a more-fluent peer, echo reading and unison reading can also be used to build fluency. A more formalized paired reading structure requires the tutor to read a short passage aloud. Then the partners read the passage together in unison several times. When the weaker reader feels ready, he/she reads the passage aloud on his/her own while the tutor provides encouragement and modeling.

Echo reading is when readers take turns reading and repeating lines of text, with one reading a line and the other echoing it.

It should always remembered that fluency is not an end in itself; it is a support for comprehension. There is no guarantee that a fluent reader will comprehend everything he/she reads, but it's pretty certain that dysfluent reading will interfere with comprehension. What we do know is that, when students can read with a degree of fluency, they will read more, read better, and enjoy it more.

Readers Theatre

Readers theatre, reader's theatre, readers' theater…there's no agreement on the spelling of the term, but there's one thing that no one disputes: this is one of the most effective processes for building reading fluency and engagement. Readers

Many free readers theatre scripts can be found online. The novel excerpts at http://www.hip-books.com/teachers/readers_theatre/ are designed especially for struggling readers.

theatre is like the radio dramas of old—no props, no costumes, no actions, and, best of all, no memorization. All the drama comes from the voices of the participants as they read individual roles from a script. Readers theatre develops comprehension by requiring students to understand and interpret characters and situations in a text (although nonfiction text also can be performed). It builds fluency through repeated reading and rehearsal. It engages both participants and audience in the performance of a shared text. And it builds confidence in even the most reluctant reader. Tim Rasinski's (2000) research reported a gain of 17 words per minute in reading speed and significant improvements in comprehension among students who engaged in readers theatre for just ten weeks.

Preparing a Readers Theatre Performance

Teaching students to read and perform a readers theatre script makes a great small-group reading unit. At first, the script is treated as any other text, focusing on comprehension, vocabulary, and the writer's craft. After studying the text, the script can be performed as readers theatre. The following steps take a readers theatre script from first reading to performance:

1. **First Reading:** If the script is at an appropriate reading level, students can read through it on their own to get an overall sense of the story and characters. If the text is a bit difficult for some of the students, the teacher might want to read the script to the students or take them through the text as a close reading.

2. **Role Assignment:** Roles can be assigned by random selection or student interest. If more than one student is interested in a role, the teacher should make a choice or draw names at random. Auditioning for roles is neither productive nor an efficient use of time for struggling readers.

3. **Script Marking:** Particularly for struggling readers, it's a good idea for each student to highlight his/her role. It's easy for readers to lose their place in a script and this helps them focus. Readers can also be encouraged to add performance notes, such as where to pause, emphasize words, or add sound effects.

4. **Individual Practice:** Repeated practice is the key to a successful readers theatre experience. Students should practice their parts aloud on their own several times until they can read their parts fluently and expressively.

5. **Group Practice:** When all students are able to read their own parts with ease, the group should come together to rehearse the entire script. It might be necessary to get group consensus on how certain parts of the script will be read. Cooperation is essential in preparing for performance. Transitions between speakers should be seamless; this is especially challenging when one speaker is called upon to interrupt another. Page turns should not interfere with the action or flow of the dialogue. In general, students should strive for as professional a performance as possible.

6. **Final Touches:** Only after the reading is polished and ready should final touches—such as music, sound effects, or even the odd prop—be added. These are incidental to the speaking parts.

7. **Dress Rehearsal:** Although readers theatre does not require costumes, the group should conduct at least one final run-through of the entire script without interruption before attempting a live performance in front of an audience. Some students might be more comfortable standing behind a podium or wearing a hat or some other prop that enables them to "hide" behind the role.

8. **Performance:** On with the show! Ensure that students have an enthusiastic audience for the performance of their readers theatre piece.

Lesson Routines to Teach the Tools of Fluency

How often have we teachers thought about actually teaching kids beyond primary grades to read out loud? In spite of the prevalence of assessments that require teachers to measure fluency with a stopwatch, there's a lot more to fluent reading than the number of words read in a minute. Reading fluency is more about pacing and phrasing than speed. Sure, we want automaticity in word recognition, but we also want readers to pay attention to punctuation, to pause for effect, to group words in phrases, and to use appropriate expression that reflects the meaning of the text. The following lesson routines focus on teaching the tools of fluency.

Punctuation Signals

Students will be able to attend to punctuation when reading orally.

Punctuation marks and font changes signal the reader to read a section of text in a certain way. Placement of commas and other punctuation marks can also affect the meaning of the text; for example, "Harry, the dog is coming after you!" has quite a different meaning than "Harry the dog is coming after you," both to you and to Harry! It is especially important for struggling readers to pay attention to signals, such as capital letters, enlarged or bold print, question or exclamation marks.

Eats, Shoots and Leaves: Why, Commas Really Do Make a Difference!; The Girl's Like Spaghetti: Why, You Can't Manage without Apostrophes!; and Twenty Odd Ducks: Why, Every Punctuation Mark Counts! are three books by Lynne Truss that share, in an entertaining, illustrated style, the ways that punctuation can change the meaning of sentences.

One way to draw students' attention to punctuation signals is to add sound effects and gestures to the reading. Many years ago, the comedian Victor Borge generated laughter simply by reading a passage and making strange sounds when there was punctuation in the text, in a schtick he called "phonetic punctuation." You and your students can make up your own sounds and gestures for each punctuation mark—or check out one of the many videos of Victor Borge online to get ideas from him. Your students are likely to find it equally hilarious to blow a "raspberry" sound and make an exaggerated pointing gesture with their finger when they encounter a period. But the most important thing is that they are learning to attend to the punctuation signals in print that tell us when to pause or change our vocal tone.

1. Display a short passage of two or three sentences for the whole group to see.
2. Identify the commas, periods, and other end-of-sentence punctuation. Suggest a sound effect and gesture for each piece of punctuation, or have students come up with ideas of their own.
3. Remind the students that, as they read the passage again, they should pause only when there is punctuation, not at the end of lines. Then read the passage chorally, using the gestures and sound effects in place of punctuation.

Must-Do Practice

Have students read a passage chorally in pairs, using "noisy punctuation." Remind students that even when they read silently, they should always be thinking about the punctuation signals that remind them to pause or change their voices.

Take a Break for Phrases

Students will be able to identify and use phrase breaks when reading aloud.

Fluent readers don't read word by word; they read in groups of words. For example, we read a phrase like "in the house" almost like one word, rather than three choppy words, "in/the/house." Sometimes punctuation marks signal phrases, but not always.

1. Reproduce a sentence or two on a visual and practice reading it together with different phrase breaks. Use slash marks to break the sentence into groups of words and try reading the phrases for expression and meaning. See sample below. You can have great fun with this, as students will see that some phrase breaks make no sense at all.
2. Talk with the students about which phrase groupings sound the best and which ones have the most logical meaning.

Teaching students to look for the signals of phrase breaks—punctuation, conjunctions, prepositions—is also an excellent reading strategy for chunking long sentences.

Sample Phrase Breaks

> How are the following two interpretations of this lengthy sentence from *Harry Potter and the Philosopher's Stone* (Rowling, 1997) different? Which one is more effective?
>
> They were the / last people you'd / expect to be /involved in anything / strange or mysterious, / because they just / didn't hold with / such nonsense.
>
> They were the last people / you'd expect / to be involved / in anything strange or mysterious, / because they just didn't hold / with such nonsense.

Must-Do Practice

Have students prepare a short passage to read aloud to the group at the next session. As they practice, they should experiment with different phrase breaks to see which ones are most effective.

Learning to Read a Script

Students will be able to read a role from a script and to describe the unique features of the text form.

A script is a unique text form that might be unfamiliar to many students. Key points to teach and practice:

- The whole story is conveyed by dialogue among a set of characters. Usually a narrator provides background information.
- The name of the character (or narrator) who speaks each line is written at the beginning of the line, sometimes in capitals, usually followed by a colon. Sometimes there are instructions for how to deliver the line, followed by the speaking part itself. Neither the character's name nor the stage directions are to be voiced, only the speech itself.
- Sometimes a line of speech is interrupted with an instruction, usually in brackets, sometimes in italics. For example, *(pause)* indicates a break in the speech and *(shouting)* tells the reader to speak loudly.

1. Show students a page of script and invite them to discuss what makes this text different from most reading that they do. As much as possible, scaffold them to discover the features of the text form.
2. Model how to read a script by noting who is speaking, how they are speaking (stage directions given, for example), and what they are saying.
3. Provide students with the opportunity to read the entire script silently before assigning roles to read it aloud.

Must-Do Practice

Assign roles and give students the opportunity to practice and present the play as a readers theatre (see page 96).

Opera Reading and Robot Reading

Students will be able to read with appropriate expression to convey the message of the text.

Expression, emphasis, and tone are the qualities of oral reading that convey meaning and engage a listener.

1. Choose an appropriate-level text and provide students with an opportunity to read it silently first.
2. Read it in chorus, in a flat and expressionless style, otherwise known as "robot reading."
3. Reread the same section of text in "opera reading," with overly dramatic and exaggerated expression.
4. After both experiences, have students talk about using appropriate expression to make their voices sound interesting and to convey the message of the text.
5. Invite students to model reading short chunks of text with expression. Then read the text again in chorus, this time with fluency and expression.

Must-Do Practice

Have students read aloud in pairs, taking turns reading sentences or paragraphs.

Poetry Performance

Students will be able to prepare and present a performance reading with fluency and expression.

Here's a learning routine that's engaging for students and terrific for building fluency: the performance reading of an interesting poem.

1. Start by providing the group with a poem. Poems by Shel Silverstein, Dennis Lee, or Jack Prelutsky are often good choices. Poems with strong rhythm and rhyme work well, but free verse can be just as effective for this routine. Read the poem together and talk about what it means. (Always focus on comprehension first!)
2. Collaboratively with students, discuss different ways to read the poem.
   - Which lines will we read chorally, which will we read in pairs, which will individuals read?
   - Where will we slow down and where will we speed up? Where will we pause for meaning or dramatic effect?
   - Where will we make our voices louder or softer?
3. Try reading the poem in different ways, for maximum interest and effect.

Must-Do Practice

Divide students into groups of three or four and provide several poems from which they can choose. The students must work together to decide how to read the poem, then practice it and perform it for the other students. It's important that students practice their poems several times and offer each other constructive feedback to improve their performances.

8

Struggling Readers Need to Read for Information

Many of our struggling readers in upper grades know how to read; they just don't know how to use reading to learn about their world. If we can just find a real grabber—a topic of interest—we can get students to use what they know as readers to learn more about that topic and, at the same time, we can sneak in some instruction about the unique strategies needed for reading to learn. We all know that pretty much everybody, even struggling readers, will go out of their way to tackle tough texts if they are motivated enough. That's why nonfiction reading is often the hook needed to reel in the indifferent reader. Whether it's about skateboarding or the supernatural, research and inquiry on topics that engage our struggling readers might just lead them to search out and even read texts that might otherwise be beyond them.

Informational reading requires all the same strategies required in narrative reading, but presents the added challenges of academic vocabulary, unique text structures, and visual features, such as tables, graphs, illustrations with captions, unique print features, and nonlinear reading.

Much of the nonfiction reading students do in school is content-area reading; in other words, science, social studies, health, and other curriculum materials. In many cases, the lines between language arts and other subjects is becoming increasingly blurred as literacy teachers incorporate more nonfiction into their programs and content-area teachers recognize the need to teach students the literacy strategies needed to access information in their subject areas. Popular buzzwords these days are "disciplinary literacy" and "academic literacy," terms used to refer to the ability to read school materials. As Vicki Zougouris-Coe (2012) asks, "How can adolescents think and learn like mathematicians, historians, or biologists if we do not teach them how to read, comprehend, and think deeply about the texts of each discipline?" Every subject area has its own unique literacy challenges. Today's mathematics class demands as much ability to read words and symbols as to read numbers. Reading social studies and history materials often requires critical thinking about the author's purpose, bias, and credibility. Science reading is full of technical vocabulary unique to the topic at hand, and is often more vulnerable to remaining current than other subject areas.

In this chapter, we'll look at routines for before, during, and after reading informational text, or info-text. Much info-text is written in a narrative style; however, unlike most narrative text forms, a page of informational text is not necessarily read in a traditional linear fashion—top to bottom, left to right. In fact, as info-texts become increasingly visual, it's not uncommon to read all over the page, in no particular order. As well, we don't necessarily need to start at page 1; we might open the book somewhere in the middle, if that's where the information we want or need is located. And if we happen to read the last page first, it's not going to give away an important plot development.

Many teachers report that their students score lower on tests of informational reading than on narrative reading. Even grade-level readers often tussle with textbooks. But most capable readers have the skill and will to struggle on, whereas a struggling reader might very well just give up, no matter how engaging the text or the topic. Our struggling readers need plenty of support and practice in the unique strategies needed for nonfiction reading. The lesson routines in this chapter are designed to provide instruction, scaffolding, and practice with informational text to enable our students to build increasing independence with reading to learn. We'll look at ideas for preparing to read, monitoring during reading, and responding after reading.

For each lesson routine, I recommend selecting texts at a manageable reading level for the students, texts that have students reading "on their tiptoes." Although we do our best to provide accessible texts during the literacy block, the reality is that sometimes our students have no choice but to read textbooks or other content-area materials that are beyond their reading level. This chapter concludes with some teacher tips for helping students navigate tough textbooks (page 111).

Before-Reading Routines

The 3 *Ps* of Prereading
- **Preview**
- **Purpose**
- **Prior Knowledge**

Readers usually choose to read nonfiction text for a purpose—because they want or need to find out something about a particular topic. Before reading, good readers often think about what they already know and what they're hoping to find out. They might glance through the passage to get a sense of whether it's likely to serve the purpose at hand. These habits are known as the 3 Ps of prereading: Preview the text, set a Purpose for reading, and activate Prior knowledge. The lesson routines that follow help students build important independent strategies for preparing to read informational text.

Map the Page

Students will be able to create a visual map of the page to locate all the pieces of information it contains.

Captioned pictures, graphs, labels, text boxes, pronunciation keys, and sidebars are intended to make informational print more interesting to readers. Unfortunately, such visuals often pose an added challenge, and even a distraction, to our struggling readers, who have been trained to start reading at the top left corner of the page and proceed to the bottom right corner. Although the body of the text is read traditionally in information text, visuals can be placed anywhere on the page and read at any point. In fact, even our best readers sometimes miss key details because of their placement on the page. Making a map of where to find all the material on the page enables readers to visualize the page and helps to ensure that they won't miss important information.

1. Choose a text that is manageable for students and has plenty of visual information. Cover one page with a sheet of acetate (e.g., an overhead transparency).
2. Talk to students about where they find the information on the page. Draw circles, boxes, or other shapes around all the chunks of information, including titles, subheadings, captions, and visuals.
3. Together, read and summarize the information found in each chunk.
4. Invite students to take a mental picture of the map so that when they read the page, they will be sure to read everything that is there.
5. You might suggest that when readers map a page, they make a plan for how they're going to read. Some people like to read the print first, while others

start by looking at the pictures and other visuals. Some readers skim the headings first; others dive right in. Make sure students know there isn't a single correct order in which to read visual text, as long as they get all the information they need.

Must-Do Practice

Provide each student with a piece of visual text, a sheet of acetate, and one or more water-soluble markers. Have them draw shapes around each chunk of text and number them in the order that they plan to read them. Remove the map from the page before reading. As students read, have them make a small check mark in the map to show that each section has been read. You might also have students write a one-sentence summary (see page 107) of the section inside each shape.

WITIK Folders

Students will be able to activate background knowledge before reading, record new learning during reading, and generate questions for further reading.

Based on Tony Stead's (2005) adaptation of the famous K-W-L (Ogle, 1986) chart, individual reading folders invite students to draw on their own background knowledge, then to confirm or reject what they think they know based on their reading. The problem with *What we Know* in the traditional K-W-L chart is that our struggling readers are often reluctant to offer ideas about what they know because they might be wrong. And, in truth, they sometimes are wrong. One of the obstacles many struggling readers face is a lack of background knowledge to support their reading, or an inability to access the background knowledge they need. Framing the task as *What we think we know* invites speculation and risk-taking.

The WITIK (What I Think I Know) folder is an excellent tool for helping students become metacognitive about activating and using background knowledge, as well as to monitor their own comprehension and learning. As always, it is expected that the WITIK process will be modeled with the whole group before students are expected to use the folders on their own. Use a large piece of chart paper folded in half to create an enlarged folder; invite students to collaboratively generate ideas before, during, and after reading. The routine that follows provides students with guided practice in using individual WITIK folders.

1. Using 8" x 11" file folders, create labels for each of the four pages: *What I Think I Know, What was Confirmed in the Reading, What I Learned,* and *What I Wonder/Expect to Learn.* (Laminating the folders preserves them a little longer, but is not really necessary.)

Although this routine is appropriate for all readers, it is more effective for struggling readers if they read the text first to get the gist of it, then reread the text to look for confirmation or new information.

2. Provide each student with an WITIK folder and a set of sticky notes in their Reading Toolkits. Before reading a selected info-text, students use sticky notes to record what they know or think they know about the topic. These are placed on the front section of the folder.
3. Have students read a short section of the text to look for confirmation of their selected facts or new information not in their folders. During or after reading, students take the sticky notes that contain facts confirmed in the reading and move them to the centre section of the folder.
4. Revisit the text to create additional stickies with new information learned in the reading.
5. The back page can be used to build anticipation before reading (What I Think I Will Learn) or to record questions for further research (What I Still Wonder).

Must-Do Practice

Provide each student with his/her own WITIK Folder and a Reading Toolkit with sticky notes. Introduce the topic of the reading and invite students to generate a number of (e.g., four to six) WITIK facts. Provide students with an appropriate-level text to read. After reading, have students move the stickies with facts that were confirmed in the reading into the inside of the folder, and add additional facts (again, you might need to require a minimum number). You might wait until students are comfortable with these steps before introducing the back cover of the WITIK folder as a place to ask questions or anticipate what the text will hold.

Get HIP to Reading

Students will be able to preview text to get an overview of the topic and text features.

HIP Preview
• Headings
• Introduction
• Pictures

Good readers often preview a text before reading to get a sense of what it is about, what's going to be most important, and what kind of demands it will place on them as readers. Probably the most important purpose of a preview is deciding whether or not to read the text. A preview can give us an indication of whether that text will serve our purposes and can also provide us with some clues about how to read the piece (see also Race-Car Reading, page 107).

The acronym HIP reminds readers of three key parts of a preview: Headings, Introduction, and Pictures. Take time to model the HIP Preview, thinking aloud to give students a sense of the process.

1. Choose a short piece of informational text that contains an introduction, a few headings, and some visuals.
2. Have students look for headings and subheadings in the text. Discuss the purpose of the headings and what information they provide.
3. Have students locate and read the introduction and talk about what they learned from this section of text.
4. Have students scan the text for pictures (any visuals, including maps, graphs, and tables). Again, talk about what information they have learned.
5. Have students read the text individually, then discuss what they learned from it. In particular, talk about how the HIP preview helped them anticipate what information would be found in the text and helped them decide how to approach the reading (e.g., difficult or easy, familiar or unfamiliar content, etc.)

6. Have students practice the strategy. Remind students that a preview is just a quick overview of the reading to get a sense of what the passage will contain and how they can prepare for reading it. They will have time to read the words in detail later.

Must-Do Practice

Although the HIP preview is intended to be a quick mental foretaste of the reading, you might want to have students complete a graphic organizer, such as the one on page 114, the first few times they try this technique, in order to practice and internalize the process.

Alphaboxes

Students will be able to organize background information and knowledge gained during reading using an alphabetical graphic organizer.

In Chapter 10, we discuss the value of graphic organizers for arranging, classifying and visualizing information, especially for struggling readers and writers. The alphabox, developed by Linda Hoyt (Hoyt, 2008), is a simple alphabetical chart that can be used to record information before, during, and after reading.

Start by modeling the use of the alphabox before expecting students to use it independently. Create an enlarged model using an interactive whiteboard or a piece of chart paper (which can be laminated and reused) and use the procedure outlined below for individual guided practice.

Teachers can use this organizer in many ways, depending on their students and their purposes for reading. Some guidelines are as follows:

- Boxes contain individual words or groups of words; sentences are not necessary.
- If a phrase or group of words is used, use the first letter of the most important word.
- Any letter box can have more than one word/phrase in it; there is no limit.
- Some letter boxes might have no words in them, if there are no significant words or ideas from the passage that begin with that letter.
- The purpose is not to fill every letter box; it's to create a visual record of the key vocabulary and concepts in the passage.

1. Choose an info-text for students to read and introduce the topic. Before reading, have students work in pairs to generate words and phrases they already know about the topic. They should write each word or phrase in the appropriate letter box.
2. Have students read the text silently to themselves. Then, with partners, they revisit the text to look for additional information to add to their alphabox. Depending on the students and the length of the passage, I'll usually establish a minimum number of words/phrases, such as ten.
3. Reassemble as a group to share the information students have gathered. Invite students to add to their own alphaboxes after the group discussion.

When students are proficient at using an alphabox organizer, they might use it to take notes during reading as well as after.

4. You might want to challenge students to scan the text a third time to find two more facts that haven't yet been discussed.

Must-Do Practice

Step 2 of the process is better completed as a must-do than in group time. After the alphaboxes are completed, students might be asked to write a summary of the key ideas in the text.

During-Reading Routines

During reading is when the real work takes place. Informational text often imposes a double burden on struggling readers: they're expected to learn and remember the content as well as processing the print. That's where tools like alphaboxes and the WITIK folder can be helpful both in the reading process and in the retention of information.

Tracking Thinking with Sticky Notes

Students will be able to notate content and process during reading.

Note that the Must-Do Practice is built into each of these routines.

As mentioned in Chapter 5, tracking thinking with sticky notes is one of the best tools for comprehension and metacognition. Here are some sticky-note tracking routines for informational text:

Knew or New?

Use sticky notes to tab facts the reader already knew and facts that are new to the reader. It might be too much work to tab every fact in the reading; you can have students tab at least two known facts and two new facts. After reading, have students share their tabbed facts with a partner. You might have pairs of students revisit the text to tab facts that were already-known and that were new to both of them.

Can This Be True?

There are many ways to use a question-mark code: "I don't get it" and "I wonder" are two. Can This Be True? involves tabbing one or two facts in the reading that might be a credibility stretch, then doing further research to corroborate the facts. In many cases, the fact is likely to be true. However, given the prevalence of Internet reading, where some material is questionable and some downright false, we want to teach students to be critical readers, to question what they read, and to seek verification when information seems even slightly questionable. After reading, discuss the Can This Be True facts and what steps the reader took to verify them.

Very Important Points

This routine, developed by Linda Hoyt (2008), helps students focus on essential ideas in the reading. Have students go back into what they have read and tab the four to six (or whatever number you choose) most important facts in the reading. Introduce this routine after the first reading of the text and ensure that students have an opportunity to discuss the facts they tabbed and why they were important. You might have students remove the notes and revisit the text with a partner to choose the six most important points on which they both agree. Then students can be asked to summarize the reading or use a text innovation, such as The Important Book on page 129.

Thinking Symbols
✓ I already knew this
+ This is new information
☆ This is really interesting or important
? I wonder
→ This reminds me of...
☺ I agree
☹ I disagree

Coding for Comprehension

As your students develop more proficiency in tracking their thinking while reading nonfiction texts, you can gradually add more codes. You and your students could create your own coding symbols and display them on an anchor chart. Place a narrow strip of removable tape along the margin of each page (or use large sticky notes) and have students put a Thinking Symbol beside each paragraph. As always, be sure to bring the group together after reading to discuss their coding and its relationship to understanding the text.

Text Features Scavenger Hunt

When reading informational text, text features can be both a support and a challenge. We can't assume that our struggling readers will know how to use a table of contents, an index, or a glossary. They need to learn that bold print, italics, and colored graphics are more than just pretty faces; they are a signal to the reader that this is featured information. Students might need help in looking at structures for how the information is organized and conveyed.

1. Use an enlarged text or provide each student in the group with a copy of a text with plenty of visual features, such as those listed at left and in the Text Features Checklist on page 116. Have students collaborate to note text features beyond the body of the text. Talk about why the author chose to use each text feature.
2. Together, create an anchor chart that lists the text features found and the purpose of each.
3. You might want to spend several days on this routine, using different texts each time, to ensure that students discover a full range of text features and solidify their understanding of each.

Must-Do Practice

Create a bookmark or checklist based on the text features your students have identified. Provide students with a piece of informational text and have them highlight special text features that they encounter. You might want to have them label each text feature with a sticky note.

Topic Sentences

A topic sentence introduces and encapsulates the information in the ensuing paragraph. The point made in the topic sentence is developed and supported by the details in the rest of the paragraph. Topic sentences not only prepare the reader for what is to come, they also guide the reader in thinking about the key ideas in, and the overall structure of, the passage. In truth, most paragraphs don't contain topic sentences (only about 13%, according to Richard Braddock's classic 1974 study), but they are useful organizers and we can have students create topic sentences for paragraphs that don't have them.

1. Demonstrate for students what topic sentences are and why they are useful to readers.
2. Display the three samples from Examples of Topic Sentence Placement on page 107 to show how topic sentences can fit into paragraphs. Explain to students that not all paragraphs will have topic sentences; however, if there is a topic sentence, it is most likely to be the first sentence of the paragraph, with supporting details following it. Explain that occasionally the topic sentence is at the end of the paragraph, and that rarely it can even be buried somewhere in the middle.
3. Suggest that students visualize a paragraph as a triangle, with the topic sentence (i.e., the point of the passage) as the point of the triangle and the

---

Students will be able to identify and use nonfiction text features.

Text Features
- Bold or colored print
- Italics
- Special punctuation: parentheses, dashes, exclamation marks
- Quotation marks not related to dialogue
- Bulleted or numbered points
- Photographs, diagrams, other images
- Captions or labels
- Pronunciation guides and definitions
- Graphs and tables
- Maps

Students will be able to identify, use, and create topic sentences in paragraphs.

Sample text is reprinted from "Winter Survival" in the HIP Teacher's Guide for *Frozen* with permission from High Interest Publishing.

supporting details as the base. Have students practice placing appropriate triangle symbols beside each (as in the sample).

Examples of Topic-Sentence Placement

<u>You don't have to go to the Arctic to deal with the dangers of cold weather</u>. In winter, much of Canada and many northern states see days with -40 degree temperatures. Add windchill, and the danger becomes that much greater.

If you have warm clothes, a sleeping bag and a way to make a fire, you can last for weeks…even a whole winter. But if you go out unprepared, the result can be disaster. <u>The key to survival is to be ready for problems</u>.

The big problem isn't cold. People have been dealing with cold weather for thousands of years. <u>The big problem is exposure</u>. If your skin is exposed to bitter, blowing wind, it can freeze in minutes. Even worse, if your clothes get wet, the chill can freeze you to death.

Must-Do Practice

Provide each student with a passage of nonfiction text that you have selected for its accessibility and its structure of paragraphs with topic sentences. Ideally, use a reproduced text that students can write on. If the text is in a book, have students place a small sticky notes along the outside margin of the page beside each paragraph. Have students draw the triangle icon that represents the structure of the paragraph beside each paragraph. They will use a *0* symbol if the paragraph has no topic sentence; have students create topic sentences for these paragraphs. At the next small-group meeting, discuss each topic sentence and how it is supportive in reading the rest of the paragraph.

One-Sentence Summaries

Students will be able to summarize the main ideas of paragraphs.

Summarizing a collection of ideas in one sentence is really giving the main idea. Identifying the main idea of a passage helps readers understand what's most important in the reading and what the author wants us to take away from it.

1. Ask students to think about a TV program or movie they saw recently and tell a partner about it in one sentence.
2. Practice with the students using a common text. Read each paragraph together, then have students work with a partner to come up with a one-sentence summary.

Must-Do Practice

Provide each student with his/her own copy of a text and have students use sticky notes to summarize each paragraph in one sentence. Place the sticky notes on the respective paragraphs and revisit them during a later class to see if students feel that they synthesized the paragraphs well enough to recall the key information.

Race-Car Reading

Students will be able to set their reading pace and style according to the purpose for reading and complexity of the text.

1. Explain to students that we read in different ways for different purposes. With dense informational text, we *putt-putt* along like an old Model T: we read every word, frequently stop to think, and even go back and reread complex information. When we're reading for pleasure, or reading easy text, we cruise along, sort of like a family sedan: reading quickly at a comfortable pace. And when we want to get a sense of what a piece of text is about or to

You can use the poster on page 117 or create your own anchor chart to draw an analogy to different car speeds.

look for a specific word or detail, we zoom along like a Formula 1 racer, running our eyes quickly over the reading.

2. Display various text samples for the group to see and talk with them about which reading speed they would use for different purposes; for example:

    a) You want to know what this text will be about so you can decide whether you want to read the whole thing.

    b) It's very important that you learn and remember all the information in this text.

    c) You read this text just because you are interested in the topic and already have lots of background knowledge on it.

Must-Do Practice

Regularly ask students about their pacing and reading style any time they tackle a piece of informational text.

Skim, Scan, or Skip?

Students will be able to use skimming and scanning, and to judge when each is appropriate to use.

Most of our struggling readers need explicit instruction and plenty of practice in fast reading (race-car reading, to use the metaphor from the preceding lesson). They tend to read every word, whether it's germane to the purpose or not. Teach students that when we want to get a sense of what a passage is about, we often *skim* a page or two to get the gist of the text. When we want to find a specific detail, we *scan* the page to search for a key word. Both processes involve running our eyes quickly over the page without focusing on individual words. Sometimes it's okay to *skip* entire chunks of text if they don't meet our purposes or provide the information we need.

1. To teach scanning, use enlarged text on a screen or chart. Model fast reading by running your finger down the page and targeting a specific word. Then give students practice by asking specific questions for them to answer by scanning the text. Talk about choosing one or two key words to focus on. You can turn it into a contest by having students compete to see how quickly they locate the required information.

2. To teach skimming, have students read a section of text quickly, running their eyes down the page. Explain that skimming is much like scanning, but this time they are reading quickly to get the gist of the passage, rather than to look for specific information. Talk with students about when to use skimming: e.g., to see if this text will be useful for our purposes, or to decide whether or not we'll be interested in reading on. Skimming might be used before reading, to establish a context for later close reading, or after reading as a quick review. Use enlarged print on a screen to display the text briefly, then remove it while students summarize what they read with a partner. Gradually increase the amount of print for students to skim (remembering that readers rarely skim more than a page or so at a time).

Some Tips for Skimming
- Read the title and introduction.
- Read the opening sentence of each paragraph.
- Look at any subheadings.
- Attend to signals of importance, such as italics or boldface.

Must-Do Practice

Have students practice scanning by providing a series of short-answer questions for them to respond to within a limited time frame. For practice in skimming, have partners skim the same section of text and then compare notes on their impressions of the text.

After-Reading Routines

What's the best after-reading routine? Read it again! The research is clear on the value of repeated reading for comprehension and fluency, not to mention to reinforce the concepts conveyed in the text (Therrien, 2004). For struggling readers (as well as for competent readers), reading the same text more than once can be a hard sell. That's why we need to make sure that there is a different purpose for reading with each repetition. Well-constructed comprehension questions (see Chapter 3) can reinforce key concepts in the reading and require students to return to the text to find evidence to support their answers. Better yet, have students use the reading for authentic research and inquiry. The routines in this section involve synthesizing information learned from the reading, through discussion, visual images, and writing.

Telegram Notes

Students will be able to take point-form notes on key ideas in reading.

When students take notes on material they've read, they learn the information more solidly and remember it longer. Unfortunately, many students don't know how to focus on only key information. How many of us, when given the opportunity to highlight "important information" in a text, end up with a sea of colored ink on the page? When teaching students how to make point-form notes, I find it helps to draw an analogy to old-fashioned telegrams, in which every word cost money. The challenge for the writer was to convey the intended message to the reader in as few words as possible.

One of the most famous telegrams was the one from Orville Wright to his father about the first successful flight of the Kitty Hawk: http://www.wdl.org/en/item/11372/

1. With students, take a look at a sample telegram. An Internet search will turn up many examples of telegrams. Discuss the message of the telegram with students and talk about what words the writer used and what he/she left out.
2. Now try the same thing with a piece of informational text. Provide a short text for shared reading. Remind students to pretend that every word costs money. Paragraph by paragraph, work together to come up with ways to convey the important information without unnecessary words.
3. Demonstrate for the students how, and work collaboratively to take point-form notes, reinforcing the concept of bulleted points as necessary, and focusing on only enough key words to help them remember each fact.
4. Try to revisit these notes a day or so later to see if students can use them to recall the important information from the text.

For detailed lesson on Telegram Notes for writing research reports, see my book *Marvelous Minilessons for Teaching Intermediate Writing*.

Must-Do Practice

Provide each student (or pair of students) with a piece of accessible text. You might want to start by providing a skeleton outline with three or four main ideas, questions, or headings, then have students fill it in with bulleted telegram notes from the reading.

Mind Maps

Students will be able to present information from text in visual form.

A mind map is a wonderful tool for organizing information, using pictures, icons, and labels (see Sample Mind Map below).

1. Tell students that a mind map contains a picture representing the main idea or topic in the middle of the page, with other pictures, visuals, or icons

(captioned as necessary) representing details about that topic radiating out from the centre.

2. Read a shared text together. Talk about what the main idea is and what the most important details are.
3. Collaboratively create a shared mind map, with all students contributing to the sketching and labeling.

Sample Mind Map

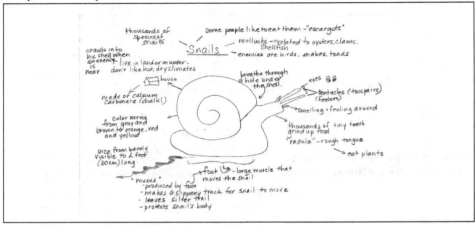

Must-Do Practice

Use a piece of informational text that students have read. Have students work in pairs or individually to create mind maps that represent the most salient details from the reading. A few days later, give students an opportunity to share their mind maps with others, showing how the visual representations helped them remember key details.

Three Facts and a Fib

Students will be able to create and identify facts and fallacies about material they have read.

This routine turns gathering information into a game, as students collect four facts from the reading and turn one of them into a "false fact."

1. Start with a common text and invite students to work in pairs to generate several facts from the reading.
2. Demonstrate how to "flip" a fact to make it false. For example, instead of "Snails breathe through a hole under their shells," you might say, "Snails have noses at the end of their antennae." Have students practice flipping the facts they have generated into false facts.

Must-Do Practice

Have students work individually or in pairs to read individual texts and generate "three facts and a fib." You might want to provide several appropriate texts from which students may choose. Have students write their facts on individual cards (illustrated if desired) and place them in an envelope. At the next group meeting, have students share their fact cards; encourage the others to compete to see who can identify the false fact. For bonus points, they can try to flip the fact back to make it true.

What If They Can't Read the Textbook?

Throughout this book, I've emphasized the importance of giving struggling readers accessible texts; that is, texts that they can read without too much difficulty, but that stretch them a bit as readers. I reiterate that the most important thing we can do to help students grow as readers is give them material that they can actually read. However, it does happen that our struggling readers are sometimes confronted with a difficult text, whether in a science textbook or a research passage. All too many textbooks are written beyond the reading ability of even readers at grade level, and often contain dull, dry, and disjointed prose. The routines already shown in this chapter are designed to build student independence. What follows are some things teachers can do to make tough texts more accessible.

> **Five Tips for Making Difficult Texts More Accessible**
> 1. Preteach vocabulary and concepts.
> 2. Provide outlines and/or anticipation guides.
> 3. Prepare the text for reading: mark key ideas and information in the text; label paragraphs or sections with subheadings.
> 4. Model how to chunk sentences and words.
> 5. Teach, practice, and reinforce strategic independence.

1. Preteach Vocabulary

We know from Chapter 2 that the two factors traditionally used in calculating the readability of a text are vocabulary and sentence length. Therefore, one important way to lower the readability of a text is to make difficult words easy. For example, the phrase "natural resources" contains two three-syllable words, and is guaranteed to raise the readability level of a 100-word passage, based on traditional measures of syllable counts. However, if we preteach that phrase and concept, we effectively reduce those words to the equivalent of simple, one-syllable words in terms of actual reading difficulty. We've already discussed the fact that preteaching more than two or three words predicts that students won't remember any of them; however, preteaching a couple of key concept words will provide the background knowledge that will enable many readers to negotiate a difficult passage of text.

2. Provide Anticipation Guides

One tool for introducing key vocabulary and concepts is an anticipation guide, a prereading task designed to help readers anticipate what they will read in the passage. We start by preparing a set of facts or concepts from the reading, some of which are factual and some of which are not. This is not only a great way to get students thinking about the concepts in the text, it also activates background knowledge, introduces key vocabulary, and sets a purpose for reading. Students are asked to anticipate which of the statements are factual, then to read on to see if they're right. After reading, readers revisit the statements to re-evaluate their veracity and, where possible, rewrite the false statements to make them true.

Anticipation Guide

1. Choose a set of important facts from the passage, incorporating key vocabulary.
2. Flip some of the facts so they are incorrect.
3. Before reading, have students read (or listen to the teacher read) the set of facts and vote on whether each is true or false.
4. After reading, revisit the facts and vote again.
5. Ask students to correct the false facts.

3. Prep the Page

In special circumstances, it might be necessary to doctor the text to make it accessible. Tricks of the trade include pre-highlighting key ideas; adding sticky-note definitions to key words; even cutting the passage up into manageable chunks. If the text has subheadings, make sure they are good predictors of the main information in that section of text; if the headings aren't supportive (or if there are no headings), create better ones that help readers anticipate the main idea of the passage. If you're reluctant to take scissors or highlighting pens to a school textbook, photocopy the section for some students.

4. Teach Students to Chunk Long Sentences

Long, complex sentences can be the ultimate challenge for dysfluent readers, who often have trouble recalling the beginning of a sentence long enough to get to the end of it. Just as we practiced chunking multisyllabic words into root words and affixes (see page 79), we can teach students to chunk sentences into clauses and phrases. Here are some chunking signals to teach students:

- *Colons and semicolons* are the most obvious signals, as they generally attach two sentences to one another.
- *Commas* often separate clauses and phrases (with the exception of serial commas that separate words in a list).
- *Conjunctions* separate coordinate clauses (conjunctions *and, but, or, so*) and subordinate clauses (conjunctions *when, because, although, if*) from the rest of the sentence.
- *Prepositions* (*after, in, to, with*) generally start phrases that indicate time or place.

Here is an example from a Grade 5 science textbook:

> As you have learned, your body breaks down the food you eat into nutrients that are dissolved in the blood and carried around the body. (*Science Everywhere 5*, Harcourt Canada, 1999)

Show students that we can use commas and conjunctions (*that, and*) to break down this 25-word sentence into four manageable chunks:

> As you have learned / your body breaks down the food you eat into nutrients / that are dissolved in the blood / and carried around the body.

You might point out the fact that the clause "as you have learned" doesn't add much to the meaning of the sentence; ask students to explain why the author might have added this clause to the sentence. If necessary, the three remaining chunks can be further broken down at the prepositional phrases: "into nutrients", "in the blood", and "around the body."

Collect some examples of complex sentences, preferably from the students' actual textbooks, for students to use in practicing chunking. It might be helpful to write these sentences on strips of paper and have students physically cut them apart. After chunking, go back and reread the whole sentences orally to practice fluency and phrasing.

5. Build Independent Learning Strategies

Although there is a range of tools teachers can use to make a specific text more manageable, ultimately students need to negotiate texts on their own. Make sure to teach and reinforce the independent comprehension strategies outlined throughout this book and the word-solving strategies in Chapter 6. Routines for previewing text, for self-monitoring during reading, for accessing challenging vocabulary, for chunking long sentences, and for synthesizing information by writing about it will not only help students access information from textbooks, it will also help them become stronger and more metacognitive readers of all informational text.

HIP Preview

Title of Passage:

HEADINGS: List three key headings you encounter in the passage and tell what you think will be found in each section.

1. _____

_____

2. _____

_____

3. _____

INTRODUCTION: Write a one-sentence summary of the information in the introduction.

_____

_____

_____

PICTURES: Briefly describe any three visuals from the passage.

1. _____

_____

2. _____

_____

3. _____

_____

Tell two things you are likely to learn from reading this passage:

1. _____

_____

2. _____

_____

© 2014 *Struggling Readers* by Lori Jamison Rog. Pembroke Publishers. ISBN 978-1-55138-292-0

Alphaboxes

A	B	C	D
E	F	G	H
I	J	K	L
M	N	O	P
Q	R	S	T
U	V	W	XYZ

© 2014 *Struggling Readers* by Lori Jamison Rog. Pembroke Publishers. ISBN 978-1-55138-292-0

Text Features Checklist

☐ Bold or colored print

☐ Italics

☐ Special punctuation: parentheses, dashes, exclamation marks

☐ Quotation marks not related to dialogue

☐ Bulleted or numbered points

☐ Photographs, diagrams, other images

☐ Captions or labels

☐ Pronunciation guides and definitions

☐ Graphs and tables

☐ Maps

© 2014 *Struggling Readers* by Lori Jamison Rog. Pembroke Publishers. ISBN 978-1-55138-292-0

Race-Car Reading

When the text is difficult or has lots of information to remember, we *putt-putt* slowly along, like an old Model T.

When the text is easy, or we're reading for recreation, we *cruise* along like the family sedan.

When we're running our eyes quickly over the page to skim or scan, we *zoom* along like a Formula 1 racer.

© 2014 *Struggling Readers* by Lori Jamison Rog. Pembroke Publishers. ISBN 978-1-55138-292-0

9

Struggling Readers Need to Read the World

No matter how much you or I might love to read, we will never convince some of our students that reading is something you do for fun. But even the most reluctant reader knows that reading is something you do to get smarter. And in the world of print in which we live, knowing how to read is always useful (reading the TV schedule or a restaurant menu), frequently necessary (reading a map or your car's owner's manual), and occasionally critical (reading instructions on a prescription or a warning sign at the edge of a cliff). Quite simply, the more you read, the more you know. And knowing how to read has become increasingly important as the demands of literacy in our world expand. These demands far exceed the ability to read the stories and novels that has traditionally dominated literacy instruction in our schools. Here we will look at a range of reading tasks in what we would consider to be nontraditional texts.

Ironically, it seems the kinds of reading we do most in the world are the kinds of reading we are least likely to teach in school. Often called *functional reading*, these texts are what enable us to function in the world. There are three main types of functional texts (and some, like brochures or websites, integrate several text forms):

- Reading to follow directions or find out how-to includes maps, recipes, manuals, and instructions or directions.
- Reading to fill out forms includes applications, entry forms, order forms, subscriptions and memberships, surveys, and, of course, taxes.
- Reading to get information ranges from schedules and timetables, advertisements, weather forecasts, and catalogues to menus and ingredient lists or labels on foods.

Although reading most types of functional text seems to come naturally to most readers, we cannot assume that even our best readers will understand all the print in their environment. Just look at how many adults don't know how to retrieve messages on their new smartphones or get lost following map directions! Just as we teach struggling readers how to navigate the intricacies of narrative text or the density of informational text, we need to teach them how to access the everyday reading that enables all of us to function in a world of print. The bonus of functional reading is that the texts are free and easy to obtain.

You might be surprised at how many of your students turn out to be struggling readers when it comes to nontraditional texts. As with other text forms, start by assessing all your students' abilities to access websites, menus, manuals, maps, and other text forms. In this way, you can determine which students will benefit

Create self-directed Functional Reading Folders with real-life text samples and accompanying generic questions and response activities for independent reading while you work with small groups of struggling readers.

most from independent learning routines and which students need some small-group scaffolding.

Of the myriad forms of functional text in our world, I've chosen to focus here on websites, schedules, instructions, store flyers, and Internet maps, with several teaching points and lesson ideas for each. Must-do practice activities are built into some of the lesson ideas, and I often recommend having students create an example of the text form as a good routine for practice. I also suggest that teachers create Functional Reading Folders, for which students help you gather examples of a particular text form. Keep the examples in a folder, along with generic and specific questions pertaining to the text samples and practice activities to engage students in reading and understanding the texts.

Reading Websites

The world-wide web has become an indispensable tool for accessing information on just about anything you would ever want to know (and a few things you wouldn't). Websites contain all the text structures and text features that paper texts contain—and more. Hyperlinks, Back buttons, and browsing-history utilities enable us to bounce all over the Net and back home, the quintessential example of nonlinear reading.

It's important to teach students the strategies for navigating a website and the potential pitfalls of using the Internet. The problem with the world-wide web is that anyone can create a website, anyone can post information anonymously, and there are no controls to ensure quality, accuracy, or even veracity of information. Unless readers are active and critical thinkers, they can be prey to false information and outright lies.

Determining credible websites and verifying information obtained from the Internet are two essential strategies for Internet reading. Internet safety is another. Recent research (Weinreich, Obendorf, Herder & Mayer, 2008) points out that most website users read a maximum of 28% of the text on the site. Skimming for specific details and scanning for a general overview of the information (see page 108) are key skills for Internet readers. Other teaching points include the following:

- Noting Text Features on a Webpage: Print a screenshot of a webpage and have students circle the features they notice (much like the Mapping the Page strategy found on page 101). Have students number the text features in the order they noticed them and talk about why some features attract our attention before others do. Talk about reading around the page rather than top to bottom, as you would a novel.
- Different Data from Different Text Features: Discuss the form each piece of information takes and whether a particular text feature is or is not the most effective way to convey that piece of information.
- Bouncing Around the Net: Discuss using hyperlinks, Back buttons, the navigation bar, and other tools to move from one webpage to another.
- Using a Search Engine: Plan instruction on how to find what you're looking for and how to decide whether a website will have reliable and accurate information.
- Completing a Webquest: The webquest is an inquiry-oriented lesson format in which most or all the information that learners work with comes from

A complete lesson plan for introducing website reading can be found in my book *Guiding Readers: Making the Most of the 18-Minute Guided Reading Lesson*.

the web. An Internet search will generate dozens of prepared webquests for students of all ages. As well, sites like WebQuest.org can guide teachers in creating webquests to correspond with their own curricula or programs of study.

Reading Schedules and Timetables

Most of us lead very busy lives that we manage thanks to schedules, calendars, and timetables. Students need to be able to read schedules in order to plan when they'll need to hand in their assignment, when they'll need to return their library books, or when their next soccer game will be. Schedules mostly tell us *when* things will happen, though they may also include information about *where* (such as concert venues), *what kind* (such as TV programs), or *how much something costs* (such as airline schedules).

Have students help you gather a collection of different schedules and timetables. Most, but not all, schedules are in the form of charts. Online schedules generally require the reader to make selections from a range of options, then follow a hyperlink to the desired schedule. For small-group instruction, teaching points might include the following:

See also Race-Car Reading on page 107.

- How to Navigate the Text Form: Some students might not know how to read a grid—moving down the vertical or across the horizontal—a calendar, or other forms of schedules.
- Purpose for Reading: Talk with students about what they might use the text form for. Ask questions: *What information can you get from this text? What information might be missing for you to fulfill your purpose? Why is or is this not the best text structure for this information?*
- Comparing Online and Print Schedules: Work with students on how to navigate an online schedule. Examine the advantages and disadvantages of print versus online schedules.
- Skimming, Scanning, Skipping: Review with students how to engage in quick reading to look for specific details or an overview of the information. Remind them that it's okay to skip some information if it doesn't suit their purposes.
- Specific Text-Related Challenges: Create prompts, questions, and exercises that require students to apply information from the text, such as *What travel options are available to you if you want to get from Toronto to Chicago? What family movies are on TV on Friday night? Where could you go to see Justin Bieber in concert?*
- Have students create their own schedules of school subjects/events or daily activities.

Reading Directions or Instructions

The website www.wikihow.com has plenty of tasks designed for young people from how to make an origami butterfly to how to get rid of acne.

My 80-year-old dad recently purchased a computer desk that included elaborate instructions for assembly. "Why do you need instructions?" he grumbled. "It's four legs and a table top." Nothing is that simple anymore! Everything seems to require instructions, whether it's how to use your new popcorn maker or how to return an item purchased online. And reading instructions requires a unique set of strategies, not the least of which is the action of following the directions to achieve the final goal.

Have students gather a collection of instructions, manuals, and directions from their homes, such as recipes, instructions for games, or electronics manuals. Make Functional Text Folders (see page 119) for independent practice.

For students who need explicit support in reading these texts, teaching points might include the following:

- Features of the Text Form: Analyze several examples of the form and note the common features, such as purpose for reading, progressive steps, sequential order.
- Reading Strategies: Note that this type of reading follows a very precise order and that following the steps in random order will guarantee that the ultimate goal will not be reached. Often the reading requires the reader to stop after each step and engage in a specific action.
- Language Features: The language in procedural text should be clear and precise. Analyze the unique structure of the imperative (command) sentence: the implied subject ("you") and the opening verb.
- Visuals: Examine any visuals and talk about whether they help readers understand and follow the directions. Talk about the relationship between the text and the visuals. Is the text supplemented, reinforced, or confused by the visuals?
- Critical Reading: Is all the necessary information in place? Is the language clear enough to follow? Is anything missing or redundant? (You might want to look at an example of procedural text that has obviously been translated from another language, to note how language confusions can disrupt the reading.)
- Compare and Contrast: Examine several different examples of procedural text and compare purpose, structure, text and print features, language, and visuals. Create an anchor chart to record the comparisons.
- Creating Procedural Text: Generate a list of topics the students are experts in, from *how to score a goal in hockey* to *how to bug your brother*. Have students write their own set of instructions.

Reading Store Flyers

Advertising is another text form that is ubiquitous in our world. Hardly a day goes by that we don't get some kind of promotional material in our mailboxes, but nothing is quite so pervasive as the flyer from the grocery store, drug store, or department store. Most of the time, these circulars go straight from the mailbox into the recycling bin, but every now and then we might be shopping for something specific. For example, I was recently in the market for a new bicycle. I had already picked out the one I wanted, but am genetically predisposed to buying only on sale. For three weeks, I scoured the store flyers to watch for the bike of my dreams to be discounted, but to no avail. At that point, I learned my dreams are pretty fickle, because I bought a different bike at a different store—but at least it was on sale.

Paper and online flyers assault the reader with images and words in bright colors and bold print, so sometimes finding what you want requires pretty serious strategic reading. It's easy to gather a collection of different store flyers for independent reading tasks; why not have students create their own challenges, questions, and prompts about the material in the flyers? For struggling readers who need additional small-group support, here are a few key teaching points:

- Critical Reading: Talk with students about the purpose for reading and the strategies readers need to use this type of text. Prompt discussion with questions: *What information is do you need to help you make an informed decision as a consumer? What information is missing? Is there information here that you don't need—that might even interfere with your purpose for reading?*
- Visual Features: Advertising flyers are essentially visual text. Ask students to glance at the page and note what information catches their eye first. Compare the information presented in words and the information presented in pictures. Note the kind of visuals that are used and invite students to speculate on why photographs are the images of choice. Talk about how the page is laid out and how this layout suits the purpose of the text form.
- Print Features: Have students look for the print on the page, noting differences in size, font, and color. Pay attention to what information is in very large print and what is in very tiny print. Introduce the term *fine print* and discuss if it carries negative connotations.
- Scanning for Details: Have students practice running their eyes over the page to look for specific information.
- Compare and Contrast: Compare two different flyers from the same type of store. Compare an online flyer with a print flyer. Create a Venn diagram or other chart to note similarities and differences.
- Using the Information: Give students a range of tasks that require them to use their reading of store flyers; for example, create a menu and have students price the items on it using a grocery-store flyer. Compare two or three stores and see which offers the best price for the same items.

See my book *Guiding Readers: Making the Most of the 18-minute Guided Reading Lesson* for additional lesson ideas for reading brochures and Internet maps.

Reading Online Maps

Personal GPS devices might soon make Internet maps obsolete, but many of us who lack map-reading skills rely on the clear and specific directions found on MapQuest or Google Maps. There are many advantages to teaching students strategies for reading these maps, not the least of which is the ability to synthesize information from diagrams, words, and symbols. Google Maps has a feature that lets you create and personalize your own maps. You can create a map of your school neighborhood to use to teach your students to become map-literate. Teaching points with online maps might include the following:

Although many of the reading processes used for Internet maps apply to print maps, print maps lack the written directions feature found in online maps; not to mention the fact that most of our students may never see a paper map in their lifetime!

- Setting a Purpose for Reading: Before reading, ask students to articulate their purpose for reading and what specific information they are looking for. Have them look at the map to find this information, then ask questions: *Is any information on this map unnecessary for your purposes? Why is it there? What background information would a reader need in order to use this map?*
- Visual Features: Draw students' attention to the visual features of the map. Talk about what information is provided in words and what information is provided in symbols and icons. Invite students to speculate about why the creators of the maps used symbols instead of words.
- Print: Note the characteristics of procedural (how-to) text: sequential order, imperative sentences, precise language. Ask *Other than the written directions, where else do you find printed words on the page?*
- Strategic Reading: Build metacognition by discussing what strategies a reader needs in order to be able to access an online map.
- Create Your Own Map: Write directions for getting between two locations on the map. Find an alternative route for locations already discussed.

10

Struggling Readers Need to Write About Reading

"If students are to make knowledge their own, they must struggle with the details, wrestle with the facts, and rework raw information and dimly understood concepts into language they can communicate to someone else. In short, if students are to learn, they must write." Graham and Hebert (2011: 2)

For many struggling readers, there's only one thing worse than reading: it's writing about reading. Ask any reluctant reader and he/she will tell you what you can do with writing—can the comprehension questions, junk the journals, and scrap the sticky notes. After all, pretty much all of our struggling readers are struggling writers. But the truth is, writing about reading is kind of like eating broccoli. You might not like it, but it's really good for you.

There is extensive research to support writing as the single best way to support reading, whether students are in Kindergarten or college (Graham & Hebert, 2011). When we write about what we read, we must reflect on the ideas in the text, connect them to our own understandings, and organize our thoughts into words on a page. Steve Graham and Michael Hebert say in their meta-analysis of the research on writing to read, "writing about a text should enhance comprehension because it provides students with a tool for visibly and permanently recording, connecting, analyzing, personalizing and manipulating key ideas in a text" (2011: 13). This is even more important with informational reading. In terms of remembering what we read, Graham and Hebert found that writing about a text was more effective than rereading it or discussing it.

The good news is that writing about reading has been shown to be particularly effective for lower-achieving students. The bad news is that if these students are not explicitly taught how to craft well-written responses, the effects on reading improvement are negligible. Good teaching is essential.

Getting It Right vs Getting It Good

One of the biggest challenges for most of our struggling readers is managing the conventions of writing—spelling, punctuation, grammar, sentence structure. And here's where we have to evaluate our priorities. In a writing workshop, surface editing and correcting the mechanics come at the last stage of a complete writing process, just before the work is published and shared with an audience. Reading responses are technically first-draft writing. Perhaps we need to back away from "getting it right" and focus on "getting it good"; i.e., putting words together so that they convey ideas with power and precision.

Modeled, Shared, and Guided Writing

Modeling may very well be the most effective tool in our pedagogical toolbox. Modeling writing enables us to show students what capable writers do, while articulating the in-the-head processes that support those actions. Using any form of enlarged print, from flip charts to interactive whiteboards, we can demonstrate how to respond to a prompt, how to support a response with evidence from the text, how to elaborate and expand on the response—and how to do all this in writing that is clear, powerful, and readable.

Levels of modeling differ, depending on the extent of teacher support and student involvement desired:

- Modeled Writing: The teacher composes aloud and writes, articulating his/ her thinking during the process.
- Shared Writing: Students collaborate to compose the text while the teacher guides and scribes, demonstrating the transfer of oral ideas to print.
- Interactive Writing: Students are involved in both the composition and scribing.
- Guided Writing: Students compose and write on their own with supports, such as writing frameworks or specific guidelines.

Written Comprehension Questions and Prompts

Believe it or not, the lowly comprehension question ranks high on Graham and Hebert's (2011) list of effective writing-to-read activities. It's important, however, that teachers craft effective questions that are clear, are concise, and lend themselves to higher-level thinking. Not only that, comprehension questions should actually require comprehension of the text. This might seem like a blinding flash of the obvious, but I've seen questions on large-scale tests that students were able to answer quite adequately without even reading the passage!

Here are some additional tips for constructing effective comprehension questions and extended response prompts:

- Craft comprehension questions so that they actually assess what you would like your students to understand. For example, a question that asks, "What does the word *chaos* mean?" tests a students' vocabulary knowledge, but might have nothing to do how well he/she has read the passage. If the question is rephrased as "What clues in the text help you understand the word *chaos*?" it assesses the reader's ability to solve a word in context.
- If you ask most youngsters a question that can be answered in one word, they will answer in one word. This is particularly true for struggling readers, many of whom tend to take everything they read literally. Be explicit: if you want the students to explain why or give evidence from the text, be sure to ask them for it.
- Don't rule out multiple-choice questions. Choosing from among a set of well-crafted responses can actually generate more critical thinking than an extended response. Take the guesswork out of multiple-choice by requiring students to explain their selections. (This is also excellent practice for large-scale assessments.)
- Make sure that the reading level of the question or prompt is not above the reading level of the text. From our knowledge of readability (see Appendix

B), we know that long sentences are one of the factors that make text difficult. Chop up long sentences into shorter ones for struggling readers. If there are multiple parts to a question, create a sentence for each; better yet, bullet each point, so that struggling readers see clearly that they are required to answer more than one part.

RAFTS

Use RAFTS to craft effective prompts. The acronym stands for

- Role of the writer
- Audience
- Format
- Topic
- Strong verb (purpose)

A RAFTS prompt asks students to take on a role, consider audience, and write for a specific purpose in a specific form. RAFTS prompts are effective for both fiction and nonfiction, as these examples show:

As Brian, write a report describing to newspaper readers how your hatchet helped you survive in the wilderness.

As Miep Gies, write a letter to your grandchildren explaining what you did to shelter the Frank family during World War II.

Here are some tips especially designed to help struggling readers respond to questions about reading:

- *Talk first, then write.* Give struggling readers a chance to formulate and rehearse their responses orally before asking them to put their ideas in writing.
- *Chill out on conventions.* Focus instead on conveying the ideas as clearly as possible.
- *Explain, elaborate, or tell why.* Teach students to do this even if the prompt doesn't explicitly ask them to. Tell them to assume that there's a *why?* in every question. You might teach them to use the FABulous Response formula shown to the left.

For a FABulous Response
Flip the question into a sentence; Answer the question completely; Back up the answer with evidence from the text.

Forms of Written Response to Reading

Personal Response

A personal response generally involves several sentences that analyze, interpret, and make connections to the text that was read. An effective written response is elaborated and well-supported with direct evidence from the text. Generally, this type of writing focuses on the text and the reader's interpretation of it, but it can also include strategies a reader uses to comprehend and interpret the text. Some types of responses:

See page 130 for a very basic holistic rubric that can be adapted for assessing many types of written response.

- Connections to personal experiences, other texts, other media, other information sources

- Interpretation of characters, events, or actions
- Description of themes or messages
- Critical analysis of author bias or point of view
- Description of writer's craft, techniques, or literary devices and analysis of their effectiveness
- Application of what was read to another situation or the larger world
- Discussion of reader's craft (strategy application, inferences, predictions, synthesis)

Think aloud as you model different kinds of responses to reading. I like to introduce this task by using a shared writing approach in which the students and I collaboratively construct the response while I do the writing. As Kylene Beers (2002) suggests, teach students key words for responding to reading; see Words That Make You Sound Smart, below. A list of sentence starters for personal response journals can be found on page 131.

Words that Make You Sound Smart

Use these terms when you're writing about reading:
- A realistic/unrealistic situation
- A suspenseful/predictable plot
- An authentic/unbelievable character
- A powerful/weak message
- Descriptive/mundane words
- A fast-moving/plodding storyline
- Unique/overdone descriptions
- Elaborated/sketchy ideas

Summarizing and Note-Taking

Our students are called upon to write summaries in many academic situations. Marzano (2001) has identified summarizing as one of the nine instructional strategies most likely to improve student achievement across all content areas and all grade levels. But summarizing is not as easy as it sounds. When asked to summarize what they've read, many students write too much or too little; they miss key information or fail to weed out insignificant details. The problem is that our students are often *assigned* to write summaries, but not often *taught* how to write them. Summarizing is a pretty demanding task for most struggling readers and writers. First, they need to be able to analyze, prioritize, and synthesize the information they have read. Then they must restate, combine, organize, and paraphrase the pieces of information.

It takes a lot of instruction and practice for our students to be able to summarize effectively. We can start with having them practice orally, inviting students to TTYN (Talk To Your Neighbor) about what happened in a recently seen TV program, movie, or even video game. Remind students that they don't tell their partners every single line of the script, but choose important details to tell. That's what summarizing is: "a shortened version of an original text, stating the main ideas and important details of the text with the same text structure and order of the original" (Kissner, 2006: 8).

Move on to practice summarizing short passages—favorite poems by Shel Silverstein or Jack Prelutsky work well. When students are able to summarize short passages, move on to larger sections of fiction and nonfiction text; i.e., chapters and even entire books.

Here are some rules for summarizing:

- Make sure to include all information that is important.
- Leave out information that's not important (extra supporting details or description).
- Put the details in the same order as they appear in the text.
- Don't repeat information, even if it's repeated in the text.
- Use key vocabulary from the text, but use your own words to craft sentences.
- Combine ideas or events that go together.
- Use category words instead of lists of words; e.g., *vegetables* instead of *carrots, beans, and corn*).

See the sample passage and teacher think-aloud below. After modeling your thinking about the passage, you might construct the summary together with students as a shared writing experience. Note that there is an added challenge in this passage, as you must convert the first-person text to a third-person summary.

Teacher think-aloud adapted from *HIP Reading Assessment* by L. Jamison (2007). This sample think-aloud also appeared in *Marvelous Minilessons for Teaching Intermediate Writing, Grades 4-6* (Rog, 2010).

Lost in the Woods

It was morning ~~and the dawn light had turned everything reddish-orange. When my heart stopped pounding, I realized that~~ I was thirsty and hungry. Even worse, those berries I'd eaten the night before weren't sitting in my stomach too well. ~~That's all I needed — to start throwing up again.~~

~~So I started off, my mouth dry and my stomach heaving.~~ I had a full day of walking ahead of me and there were two people back at the crash site who were depending on me. I was determined to keep on going, ~~no matter how queasy I felt.~~

I came across water two hours later. ~~It was only a small stream, but as far as I was concerned, it was the best water I'd ever tasted.~~

By afternoon, I was so starved ~~I would have eaten my shoes.~~ I decided to risk some of the berries again, despite what they did to my stomach.

By sundown, I was exhausted and had been eaten alive by bugs. ~~If a bear had come by, I wouldn't have had any fight left in me. But no bears came even close, although I saw a few of them in the distance.~~ I sat down under a pine tree, ~~looked up at the dying light~~ and wondered if I'd ever make it home again.

I think the time of day is important but the rest is extra description – interesting, but not important. I don't need to include heart pounding. I can just tell that the character is thirsty and hungry and not feeling too well.

The first sentence just repeats what we already know – he's sick and thirsty. But the rest is important! There are two people at the crash site who need him, so he has to keep walking.

Finally he finds water to drink. By afternoon, he's so hungry he decides to eat the berries, even though they made him sick the night before.

By sunset, he's exhausted and bitten by bugs. He wonders if he'll ever get home again.

There are different ways to summarize this passage, but here's one example:

In the morning, the character is hungry and thirsty and doesn't feel well. But he needs to keep going because two people at the crash site need him. He finally finds some water to drink, but by afternoon, he is so hungry that he eats some berries, even though they made him sick the night before. By nighttime, he is exhausted and bug-bitten and wonders if he's ever going to get home.

From Retelling to Summary

One way to teach summarization is to start with retelling and to condense the retelling into a summary. Retelling involves recounting every salient detail in the order it occurred in the reading, using as much vocabulary from the text as possible; summarizing involves stating only key ideas and using your own words as much as possible. To teach the process, walk students through a retelling of a familiar piece of text. Try to include every single detail, whether it's important or not. Then, with the students, go through the retelling statements to combine or delete them as needed to create a summary. Familiar fairy tales are good texts to use for this routine.

Other Summarizing Routines and Activities

- Very Important Points: When reading nonfiction, have students highlight or use sticky notes to tab VIPs, or Very Important Points (Hoyt, 2008). (You might want to set a required number of points, depending on the length of the text.) Start with a topic sentence, then use these VIPs to create a summary of the information in the passage. See page 132 for a VIP graphic organizer.
- Sticky-Note Summaries: Give each student a 3" x 5" sticky note on which to summarize a given passage. Then give each student a 3" x 3" note to condense the summary further. Finally, give each student a small 1" x 1" sticky to write a one-sentence summary or main idea.
- Somebody…Wanted…But…So…: SWBS is a time-honored tool for summarizing the plot of a story. Most story plots boil down to this simple structure: a character (somebody), a problem or goal (wanted), an obstacle (but), and a resolution (so). See page 133 for the a graphic organizer that can be used to write this kind of summary. Here's an example of an SWBS summary:

  Charlotte wanted to help Wilbur but Mr. Arable was going to have him slaughtered, so Charlotte spun words in her web in Wilbur's pen and Wilbur's life was saved.

- Two Key Words: This strategy, adapted from Linda Hoyt (2008), works particularly well with nonfiction text. Have students read a paragraph of informational material, then select two key words to represent the most important ideas. Students should talk to a partner or to the group about which words they chose, why they chose those words, and what the words mean to the passage.
- The Important Thing: Margaret Wise Brown's classic picture book *The Important Book* offers a simple template for scaffolding struggling writers as they learn to summarize texts. They start by identifying the main idea of the topic, then add three or four supporting details. See template on the next page.

Teaching readers to summarize the plot of a novel using the SWBS structure helps them focus on the key ideas and guides them to navigate other fictional narrative reading with a more informed stance as a reader.

The Important Thing About _____

The thing about _____ is _____.

It/They _____.

It/They _____.

And it/they _____.

- Another Point of View: Tell what happened in the story or an event from the story from the point of view of another character.
- A Different Text Form: Write a summary in a text form other than the original; try a free-verse or patterned poem, a biographical sketch, a procedure (how-to), a labeled diagram or mind map, a news article, etc.
- Storyboards: Let's not forget visual summaries! Have students fold a piece of paper in four and sketch and label four key events or facts from the reading. Remember that a drawing in response to reading is not expected to be fine art. It's less about beautiful pictures and more about communicating ideas in a visual manner.
- Twitter Summaries: Challenge students to summarize a chapter or short text in 140 characters or less!

Graphic Organizers

Graphic organizers are visual and verbal representations that create networks of ideas in different structures, including outlines, mind maps, and story grammars. Graphic organizers have been shown to support reading comprehension and vocabulary development for learners at all levels (Moore & Readence, 1984), but they are particularly supportive of struggling readers. Graphic organizers help readers categorize and organize their ideas by providing a visual, at-a-glance overview of key information. And they reduce the intimidation factor by limiting the amount of writing that needs to be done. (There's something about writing in a box that is more manageable than writing on a blank piece of paper!) It should be noted, however, that the efficacy of graphic organizers is contingent on effective teacher modeling and instruction (Gardill & Jitendra, 1999).

Organizing information and noting relationships between ideas are common challenges for many readers. Graphic organizers guide readers and writers in distinguishing key information from supporting details, in representing ideas both visually and verbally, and in noting connections and contradictions between new ideas and existing knowledge.

The world's simplest graphic organizer is a piece of paper folded into two parts. This two-column chart may be used for a variety of purposes, including

- What I Wonder/What I Think
- Inferences/Evidence from the Text
- What the Text Says/What I Think
- Main Ideas/Supporting Details
- What the Text Says/My Connections
- My Predictions/Evidence from the Text
- Key Word/Definition

Note that any of the organizers from pages 134 to 140 can be adapted for different readers by increasing or reducing writing requirements.

Pages 134 to 140 contain teacher-tested and pupil-proven graphic organizers for writing about reading. It's very important to demonstrate how to complete these organizers and to provide students with plenty of opportunities for guided practice before expecting them to complete the organizers on their own. However, once students have mastered some of these generic graphic organizers, they will have a repertoire of tools to support writing in a range of reading situations.

- Excitement Graph, page 134: This graphic organizer illustrates how stories develop. Not only does this organizer help students think about rising and falling action in a story but, when completed, it gives a clear picture of rising and falling action in a story.
- Story Staircase, page 135: Like the Excitement Graph, this organizer reflects story grammar, or the structure of a story.
- Character Chart, page 136: On this graphic organizer, students are asked to identify traits of a character and to record specific support from the text.
- Story Pyramid, page 137: Students must summarize the story using lines of limited words. This is a good organizer for students to complete in pairs, as they need to need to negotiate what words to use in order to convey their ideas most effectively.
- Be a Reporter, page 138: This graphic organizer requires students to analyze a character from the reading by generating a set of questions in order to interview the character, then writing the character's possible answers.
- Retell, Relate, Reflect, page 139: This three-part written response (Schwartz & Bone, 1995) asks for a brief summary of the reading, a connection to the reader or real life, and the reader's reflections on the reading.
- SOS (Summary, Opinion, Support), page 140: Students are asked to write a brief summary of the reading, then an opinion about the content or the writer's craft.

Assessing Written Responses

What makes a good written response? First, it should address the question or prompt and reflect an understanding of the reading. Second, it should make specific reference to the text. Higher-level responses—with insight and elaboration—generate higher-level scores. Here is a very basic rubric that can be adapted to many different written response tasks.

Assessing Written Responses

5 Points	4 Points	3 Points	2 Points	1 Point
Thorough and well-crafted response that extends beyond the obvious or expected and includes strong support from the text	Thorough response with strong support from the text	Credible response with limited support from the text	Marginal response that reflects some comprehension of the text but lacks elaboration or support	Response reflects negligible understanding of the reading and/or the question asked

Sentence Starters for Response Journals

Do you need some help giving your response journal a kickstart? Try these sentence starters to get your mind in gear and your pen moving.

- This reading made me think of….
- If I could change one thing, it would be…
- Here's how my thinking changed from the beginning to the end:…
- I wonder…
- My big question about this reading is…
- If I were the character…
- The character…reminded me of …
- As I read, I realized that…
- I wish…
- What I learned from this reading was…
- The most important part of this reading was…
- Something the author did really well/poorly was…
- I was confused by…
- I can tell that the author thinks…
- If this book was a movie…
- I agree/disagree that…
- This book is most appropriate for boy/girl/older/younger readers because…
- If I could step into the story, I would…
- The most interesting character was…
- I think that the author wants the reader to…

© 2014 *Struggling Readers* by Lori Jamison Rog. Pembroke Publishers. ISBN 978-1-55138-292-0

VIP Chart

In each of the the four VIP boxes, write a Very Important Point from your reading. Use those facts to write a summary in the middle box.

VIP	**SUMMARY** **Topic Sentence:** _____ _____ _____ **Summary of Key Ideas:** _____ _____ _____ _____ _____ _____ _____ _____ _____ _____ _____	VIP
VIP		VIP

© 2014 *Struggling Readers* by Lori Jamison Rog. Pembroke Publishers. ISBN 978-1-55138-292-0

SWBS Chart

SOMEBODY…WANTS…BUT…SO…

Did you know that almost all fiction stories follow a similar structure? A character wants to solve a problem or achieve a goal, but something gets in his or her way, so the character has to overcome a challenge.

SOMEBODY (Tell something about the main characters)

_____ is a _____

who _____ .

WANTS (What is this character's problem or goal?)

_____

_____ .

BUT (What happens to get in the character's way?)

_____

_____

SO (How does the character resolve the problem and end the story?)

_____

_____

© 2014 *Struggling Readers* by Lori Jamison Rog. Pembroke Publishers. ISBN 978-1-55138-292-0

Excitement Graph

Along the bottom of the page (the left side of the graph), retell the story, event by event, in 8 to 10 sentences. Then create bars by filling in the boxes to show how exciting each event was.

Level of Excitement

10
9
8
7
6
5
4
3
2
1
0

Events from the Story

Title _____

Author _____

© 2014 *Struggling Readers* by Lori Jamison Rog. Pembroke Publishers. ISBN 978-1-55138-292-0

Story Staircase

Starting at the bottom, record the problem and the most important events in the story.

How does it end?

What's the most exciting part?

What happened next?

What happened next?

What happened first?

What's the problem?

© 2014 *Struggling Readers* by Lori Jamison Rog. Pembroke Publishers. ISBN 978-1-55138-292-0

Character Chart

Write the character's name in the centre oval. In each of the small rectangles, write one thing you know about the character. In the larger boxes, tell how you know by giving proof from the story.

© 2014 *Struggling Readers* by Lori Jamison Rog. Pembroke Publishers. ISBN 978-1-55138-292-0

Story Pyramid

Name _____

Summarize the story by choosing key words and phrases and placing them in the rows.

One word: name the main character
Two words: describe the main character
Three words: describe the problem
Four words: the first event in the story
Five words: the second event in the story
Six words: how the problem is solved

Book Title

_____

_____ _____

_____ _____ _____

_____ _____ _____ _____

_____ _____ _____ _____ _____

_____ _____ _____ _____ _____ _____

© 2014 *Struggling Readers* by Lori Jamison Rog. Pembroke Publishers. ISBN 978-1-55138-292-0

Be a Reporter

Reporters know how important it is to ask "thick" questions, questions that can't be answered in just a word or two.

Choose one of the characters from your story to interview.

Make up five good questions to ask the character. Then pretend you're the character and answer the questions the way you think that character would.

Interview with _____ (Character)

Question	Answer

© 2014 *Struggling Readers* by Lori Jamison Rog. Pembroke Publishers. ISBN 978-1-55138-292-0

Retell, Relate, Reflect

RETELL	*This is about…* *The most important part was…*
RELATE	*This reminds me of…* *This is similar to/different from…*
REFLECT	*I wonder…* *I think…* *I noticed…* *I agree/disagree with…*

© 2014 *Struggling Readers* by Lori Jamison Rog. Pembroke Publishers. ISBN 978-1-55138-292-0

SOS

In the real world, SOS is a call for help, but in this graphic organizer it's a way of organizing our thinking about reading: **S**ummarize the text, give an **O**pinion about it, and add **S**upport for your opinion.

Write a 2–3 sentence SUMMARY of your reading:

Express an OPINION about the reading:

Provide SUPPORT for your opinion:

Some Ideas for Opinions

- What do you think of the characters? Are they believable? Do you agree or disagree with something they have done or said?
- What do you think about the problem or plot? How else might it have been resolved? Was the ending satisfactory? How might you change the ending?
- What kind of response did you have to the reading? Was it funny, sad, interesting, exciting, or dull?
- What do you think about the author's writing? Were there examples of really effective or ineffective word choice? Did the action move along at the right pace?

© 2014 *Struggling Readers* by Lori Jamison Rog. Pembroke Publishers. ISBN 978-1-55138-292-0

Conclusion: What Struggling Readers Need Most

Sometimes programs, innovations, and techniques work with some struggling readers. At other times, the same programs, techniques and innovations don't work. What makes the difference? Teachers do. As Hall and Harding say, "Many curriculum approaches and packages have been found both to work and to fail: what seems critical is the skills of the teacher" (2003:1). Teachers are central to the delivery of effective teaching of reading. They need know their students, their pedagogy, and their resources. They need to be well-trained, be well-supported, and, perhaps most important of all, have positive relationships with their students.

My husband is a former high-school teacher and author of many novels for young adult readers, and often tells this story. A teacher who was introduced to him said,

> "I need to thank you for saving my life. When I was young I was a struggling reader. People thought I was dumb and so did I. But in Grade 5, my teacher brought me one of your books and told me, 'I think you might enjoy this book.' I took it home and was so excited that I was able to read it. It was the first book I had ever read right through. So I asked my teacher for another Paul Kropp book, and another, and another. Suddenly, I was a reader! Eventually I moved on to a lot more books and a lot more authors, but it was your books that saved my life."

Paul replied, "I appreciate your thanks, but I wasn't the person who saved your life. It was a teacher who knew you and cared about you enough to put the right book in your hands at the right moment. She's the one you should be thanking, not me."

You want to be the teacher deserving that thanks. You want to be the teacher who rescues students' reading lives. And you can be. That's why we teach.

Appendix A: Book Excerpt

CHAPTER 1

The Bet

It started with me shooting off my mouth. The four of us were walking down Barton Street on the way to school. I was with my little brother, Zach, like always. A.J. and Hammy were going down the street with us, A.J. riding on his bike and Hammy with his skateboard.

We were goofing around, like always, when we passed the old Blackwood place. It's a big old house that used to belong to this lumber guy, back when

our town was full of lumber mills and the river chock full of logs. I guess the house must have been pretty nice back then. These days it's all boarded up, with half the roof sagging and the paint all peeled away.

"It's haunted, you know," A.J. said. His real name is Alexander, but we've called him A.J. ever since we were little kids.

"Riii-ight," I replied. "And I'm really King Tut come back to life."

"No, I'm not kidding," A.J. went on. "My dad says that a kid got stabbed in there years ago. And I've been by here at night and you can still see funny lights moving around inside." He sounded all pumped up, like he was actually scared.

"Must be some high-school kids having a party," my brother Zach told him, "trying to find some place to crash where the rats won't get 'em."

Hammy zoomed up the sidewalk to the steps on his skateboard, then did a 180 ollie that looked pretty slick. "Hey, ghosts!" he shouted. "How do you like that? You want to see me do a grind?"

"See?" I told A.J. "The ghosts didn't say a thing.

They didn't even give Hammy a round of applause. If that place is haunted, how come the ghosts are so quiet?"

"It's quiet as a tomb," my brother threw in. He made his voice real deep for the "tomb" part, sort of like TOOOM!

"You guys shouldn't joke," A.J. came back. "There's more to this world than you and me understand."

"Like ghosts?" I asked. "How about witches and warlocks and frogs that turn into princes?"

"But only if they're kissed, right?" my brother added. Then the three of us all broke into big laughs.

Laughing is what the four of us do best. We'd been laughing together ever since . . . well, ever since ever. We were together in preschool, friends in grade two and best buddies since grade six. Except my brother, of course. He's not my friend because he's my brother, and because he's a dork sometimes. But still, the four of us are always hanging together. If ever there is a ball game, we become half the team. If there is a movie to see, we

all go together. If there is a problem, then all of us have to fix it. Like the time Hammy's line drive smashed Mrs. Headly's window. We all chipped in on that one. After all, it was my baseball, A.J.'s bat and Zach's pitch that got the ball going. We are that tight.

But that doesn't mean we always agree on stuff. Hammy, for instance, takes school very seriously. He studies all the time, which is funny for a skater. A.J. is really the jock in our group. He follows all the sports there are, even golf, and he plays half of them pretty well. My brother, well, he's just a junior version of yours truly. Except that about a year ago he got the same size as me. People think we're like twins. Teachers at school call us double trouble: "Here come the McCann brothers. Better watch out."

Not that we're bad, really. Just a bit smart mouth, sometimes.

"You guys should listen up," A.J. said. He was getting that serious voice, like we were about to make some big mistake. "Somebody got killed in that house, way back when. My dad told me about

Excerpt from *Ghost House* by Paul Kropp reproduced with permission from High Interest Publishing (www.hip-books.com). Permission to copy for classroom use.

it. People say it's been haunted ever since. That's why no one will buy it. The place has a curse on it."

"Whooooo! Whoooooo!" my brother said, then began laughing.

"Heaven protect us!" I shrieked.

"You guys make me so mad," A.J. told us. "Halloween is coming up, and there's no telling what might happen. Stuff isn't as simple as you think."

I shook my head and looked hard at him. "A.J., there are no ghosts, anyplace. There's just no such thing. When you're dead, you're dead," I said. They were the same words my dad used to say.

"Unless you're a mummy!" my brother shouted, and then he began walking with his arms out, mummy style. We'd done that for a play last year for the little kids in grade two. They thought it was great.

A.J. got a funny look on his face, then smiled at the two of us. "OK, if you guys are so brave, I've got a deal for you. Spend one night in the Blackwood house – one full night – and I'll . . . ." His voice trailed off.

"You'll what?" I asked, challenging him.

8

"I'll give you fifty bucks," he concluded.

"Fifty bucks to spend a night with cobwebs and rats?" I replied. "You've got to be kidding! How cheap do you think we are? We could make almost that much babysitting."

"OK, so how much?" he asked.

I turned to my brother, Zach. We both knew that A.J. was the guy with money. He was the one with the big-screen TV at home and the fancy Lexus in the drive. A.J. gets more money for allowance than my sister gets working at Sobeys.

"A hundred . . . each," Zach said. He drives a hard bargain. I think he'll go into business some day and make millions.

The money made A.J. stop and think. Two hundred bucks is a lot of money. For a kid in grade eight, like us, it's a ton of money. We knew that A.J. had the cash. I once saw his savings account passbook, and he had a good five thousand just sitting in the bank. But would he take the bet?

"Deal," A.J. replied. He turned to Hammy so he'd listen up and then laid down the terms. "A hundred, each. You've both got to stay inside for 12

9

hours, like seven to seven. No leaving. No sending out for pizza. You come out even once, and you lose. And if you lose, then you've got to give me that baseball you've got, the one autographed by Mark McGwire."

"No way," we both shouted.

"That's a World Series ball," I said, though A.J. knew it full well. "Our dad got that for us. I mean, you've got to be dreaming to think we'd ever give that to you."

10

"OK, so you loan it to me, for a month."

"Just a month. And no touching it too much," I said.

"What, you backing out? You think you might lose the bet? I thought you guys had some guts."

I looked over at Zach. We were both thinking the same thing.

"We're not backing out," I replied. "We're in – Hammy is the witness. Two hundred bucks versus the Mark McGwire ball."

"Deal," A.J. replied.

"Deal!" I said, holding out my hand to shake his. "Kiss the money goodbye, A.J."

11

Appendix B: Oral Reading Assessment

1. Prepare the materials

Before beginning the assessment, prepare all the materials. Make copies of each of the grade-level passages. (Some students might read through several grade-level passages before you find their instructional reading level.) Have several copies of each of the teacher record sheets in a file or three-ring binder.

2. Prepare the room

Place a table and two chairs in a spot where neither you nor the reader will be distracted by other students. Be sure that other students will not be able to hear the reading and questioning. Some teachers prefer to administer the assessment in another room or in the hallway outside the classroom. Others are able to isolate a corner of their regular classroom.

3. Prepare the other students

Provide productive independent or small-group activities for the rest of the students. If you have not yet established independent work routines in your classroom, it might be necessary to demonstrate and practice the following procedures:
- what to do if students have a question
- what to do if student are stuck on something
- what to do if students have finished their activity

4. Determine where to begin

By the end of September, you will likely have a sense of the reading abilities of most of your students. Use that professional judgment to determine a starting point for each student's assessment. Start with a passage you believe will be easy for the student and will build confidence and comfort with the process. Then move on to a passage more likely to be at the student's instructional level.

5. Introduce the assessment

Do your best to alleviate any anxiety on the part of the student and reassure him/her that the information from the assessment will be used to help you plan your teaching to help him/her grow as a reader. Remind the student that this isn't for a mark and there's no way to fail. Encourage the student to try his/her best and use whatever strategies he/she knows to read the words and respond to the questions. Tell the student that he/she will be asked to read part of a passage out loud to you. Then you will ask him/her some questions about what he/she understood about the passage.

6. Have the student read the passage aloud

As the student reads aloud, record miscues. It might be helpful to sit slightly behind the student or in some other position that does not distract the student as you write.

Assisting or providing a word during an oral reading record are discouraged. If the student pauses for an inordinate length of time (i.e., more than 3–5 seconds), gently prompt by suggesting that he/she "just give it a try" or "take a guess." If the student is simply unable to go on, tell him/her the word and note it as a *T* or teacher-assisted. Avoid the temptation to teach or scaffold. As the student reads, take note of reading behaviors, such as finger pointing, lip movement, vocalization, or inappropriate reading speed.

7. Determine the reading level

- If the student's word accuracy is 90% or higher, continue with the comprehension assessment.
- If the reader makes ten miscues in a passage, it is clearly at the student's *frustration* level. Stop the reading and move to an easier passage. Frustration-level reading should not be continued.
- If the passage reading was nearly flawless, go to a more difficult passage.

8. Do a comprehension assessment

Even if the passage is at the student's independent level, do not skip the comprehension check. Some students can read a text with accuracy but fail to comprehend it adequately.

After the oral reading section is complete, have the student reread the passage silently before responding to a comprehension assessment. Feel free to prompt the student if a response is incomplete or lacking support from the text; for example, *Can you tell me a little more?* or *What does the text say that makes you think that?*

9. Determine instructional reading level

Move to a higher or lower level passage and repeat the process until you have determined the student's instructional reading level based on a combination of accuracy and comprehension.

Appendix C: Readability

What makes a text easy or hard to read? Some tools for judging the amount of challenge presented by a given text include traditional readability formulas and the more recent systems of leveling books, or defining their text gradients.

Leveling systems use criteria, such as illustrative support, predictability, print features, language and literary features, and text structure, to distinguish one level from another. These systems are somewhat arbitrary and are more useful for texts for younger students; however, a consideration of these criteria provide us with useful information about what types of supports and challenges a particular text will offer a reader.

Readability formulas use mathematical calculations to assign a grade-level score to texts, based on the lengths of the words and the length of the sentences. Most formulas have no way of judging the difficulty of a word for a particular reader (although the Dale-Chall Formula factors in words that do not appear on their list of 3000 "common" words), so they use a syllable count to determine the average word length, on the assumption that longer words are more difficult to read.

> **Test It Yourself**
>
> Your computer can measure the readability of a passage for you! In MS Word, under Spelling and Grammar, you can choose "Show readability statistics." After you have run the grammar checker, Word will provide a grade-level readability analysis based on the Flesch-Kinkaid formula.
>
> Another useful tool is the Juicy Studio website, which provides information on readability analyses for print and websites: juicystudio.com/services/readability. php#readweb

We all know that there are limitations to these formulas. Many multi-syllabic words are common and quite decodable; for example, *transportation, computer,* or *electricity*. Try tossing my home town of Saskatoon, Saskatchewan, into a 100-word passage and watch the readability shoot through the roof! Yet it shouldn't present any great challenge to anyone, even struggling readers, who live in that city. By the same token, even one-syllable words like *angst, stave,* or *spiel* might be unfamiliar to many young readers.

Just as with leveling systems, readability systems tell us only what challenges the books bring to the situation. It takes a wise teacher, with good knowledge of his/her students, to factor the reader into the reader–text equation. For example, based on an oral reading record, let's say you have determined that Grade 3.5 readability is the appropriate instructional level for a particular sixth-grader. However, that doesn't mean that just any passage at a mid–Grade-3 reading level will be appropriate for that particular student. We need to use our professional judgment to determine whether that text will be interesting, engaging, and comprehensible to him or her. We need to ask ourselves the following questions:

- How many challenging words in the passage is this reader likely to struggle with? (For example, are the words *Saskatoon, Saskatchewan* likely to be a breeze or a bugaboo?)
- What is the concept load of this passage? Is the reader likely to have the necessary background knowledge to understand the material?
- Are the text structure and text features likely to add an additional challenge for this reader? For example, are there charts and tables, maps, or other text features that might be unfamiliar? Are there flashbacks or foreshadowing or other literary elements that could be confusing to a literal reader?
- Is the reader likely to be interested in the topic and motivated to read this material?

Fortunately, there is much to choose among children's and young-adult print literature, educational texts, the world-wide web, and the many forms of functional text in the world around us. As long as we understand a bit about the art and science of readability, about the features of a text that make it more or less challenging, and about the needs and interests of our students, we will be able to help our students find those just-right texts that will help them grow as readers.

Resources

Professional Resources

Alexander, P., Graham, S., & Harris, K.R. (1996) "A Perspective on Strategy Research: Progress and prospects" *Educational Psychology Review*, 10, 129–154.

Allington, R. (2001) *What Really Matters for Struggling Readers*. New York, NY: Addison-Wesley Educational.

Allington, R. (2009) *What Really Matters in Response to Intervention*. Boston, MA: Pearson.

Anderson, R.C., Wilson, P.T. & Fielding, L.G. (1984) "Growth in reading and how children spend their time outside of school" *Reading Research Quarterly*, 23, 285–303.

Anglin, J. (1993) *Vocabulary Development: A Morphological Analysis*. Chicago, IL: University of Chicago Press.

Beck, I., McKeown, M. & Kucan, L. (2013) *Bringing Words to Life, 2nd Ed.* New York, NY: Guilford Press.

Beers, K. (2002) *When Kids Can't Read: What Teachers Can Do*. Portsmouth, NH: Heinemann.

Bereiter, C. & Bird, M. (1985) "Use of Thinking Aloud in Identification and Teaching of Reading Comprehension Strategies" *Cognition and Instruction*, Vol. 2, No. 2, 131–156.

Bereiter, C. & Scardamalia, M. (2004) *Technology and Literacies: From Print Literacy to Dialogic Literacy*. Toronto, ON: OISE.

Betts, E. (1946) *Foundations of Reading Instruction*. New York, NY: American Book Company.

Biemiller, A. (2001) "Teaching Vocabulary: Early, direct, and sequential" *American Educator*, 25(1), 24–28.

Botzakis, S. (2009) "Graphic Novels in Education: Cartoons, comprehension and content knowledge" in Wooten & Cullinan (Eds.) *Children's Literature in the Reading Program*. Newark, DE: International Reading Association.

Braddock, R. (1974) "The Frequency and Placement of Topic Sentences in Expository Prose" *Research in the Teaching of English*, Winter 1974.

Chall, J., Jacobs, V. & Baldwin, L. (1991) *The Reading Crisis: Why Poor Children Fall Behind*. Cambridge, MA: Harvard University Press.

Common Core State Standards Initiative (2010) *Common Core State Standards for English Language Arts and Literacy in History/Social Studies, Science, and Technical Subjects*. Washington, DC: National Governors Association Center for Best Practices & Council of Chief State School Officers.

Cotton, K. (1988) *Classroom Questioning.* Education Northwest School Improvement Research Series: educationnorthwest.org/webfm_send/569

Cunningham, A. & Stanovich, K. (2001) "What Reading does for the mind" *Journal of Direct Instruction* 1:2, 137–149.

Cunningham, P. & Hall, D. (1998) *Month by Month Phonics for the Upper Grades.* Greensboro, NC: Carson-Dellosa.

Duke, N. & Pearson, P.D. (2002) "Effective practices for developing reading comprehension" in Farstrup, A. & Samuels, J. (Eds.) *What Research Has to Say about Reading Comprehension.* Newark, DE: International Reading Association.

Elbaum, B., Vaughn, S., Hughes, M., Moody, S. & Schumm, J. (2000) "How Reading Outcomes of Students with Disabilities Are Affected by Instructional Grouping: A meta-analytic review" in Gersten, R., Schiller, E. & Vaughn, S. (Eds) *Contemporary Special Education Research: Syntheses of the Knowledge Base on Critical Instructional Issues.* London, UK: Routledge.

Farr, R. & Conner, J. (2004) "Using Think-Alouds to Improve Reading Comprehension" from LD Online: http://www.ldonline.org/article/102/.

Fountas, I. & Pinnell, G. (2001) *Guiding Readers and Writers Grades 3–6.* Portsmouth, NH: Heinemann.

Frayer, D., Frederick, W.C. & Klausmeier, H.J. (1969) *A Schema for Testing the Level of Cognitive Mastery.* Madison, WI: Wisconsin Center for Education Research.

Gambrell, L. (2011) "Seven Rules of Engagement: What's most important to know about motivation to read" *The Reading Teacher,* 65:3, Nov 2011.

Gardill, M.C., & Jitendra, A.K. (1999) "Advanced Story Map Instruction: Effects on the reading comprehension of students with learning disabilities" *The Journal of Special Education,* 33(1), 2–17.

Ganske, K., Monroe, J. & Strickland, D. (2003) "Questions Teachers Ask about Struggling Readers and Writers" *The Reading Teacher,* 57:2, October 2003, 118–28.

Gavigan, K. (2011) "More Powerful than a Locomotive: Using graphic novels to motivate struggling male adolescent readers" *The Journal of Research on Libraries and Young Adults* http://www.yalsa.ala.org/jrlya/2011/06/more-powerful-than-a-locomotive-using-graphic-novels-to-motivate-struggling-male-adolescent-readers/

Gavigan, K. & Tomasevich, M. (2011) *Connecting Comics to Curriculum: Strategies for Grades 6–12.* Santa Barbara, CA: Libraries Unlimited.

Gear, A. (2006) *Reading Power.* Markham, ON: Pembroke.

Goodwin, A.P., & Ahn, S. (2010) "A Meta-analysis of Morphological Interventions: Effects on literacy achievement of children with literacy difficulties" *Annals of Dyslexia,* 60, 183–208.

Gorman, M. (2003) *Getting Graphic! Using Graphic Novels to Promote Literacy with Preteens and Teens.* Santa Barbara, CA: Linworth.

Graham, S. & Hebert, M. (2011) *Writing to Read: Evidence for How Writing Can Improve Reading.* New York, NY: The Carnegie Corporation

Graves, M. (2009) *Teaching Individual Words: One Size Does Not Fit All.* New York, NY: Teachers College Press/IRA.

Guthrie, J.T., & Wigfield, A. (2000) "Engagement and Motivation in Reading" in M.L. Kamil, P.B. Mosenthal, P.D. Pearson, & R. Barr (Eds.) *Handbook of Reading Research, Volume III.* New York, NY: Erlbaum.

Hall, R. (1984) *Sniglets (Snig'lit: Any Word That Doesn't Appear in the Dictionary, But Should).* New York, NY: Macmillan.

Hart, B. & Risley, T. (1995) *Meaningful Differences in the Everyday Experience of Young American Children.* Baltimore, MD: Brookes Publishing.

Harvey, S. & Goudvis, A. (2007) *Strategies That Work (2nd Edition).* Portland, ME: Stenhouse.

Hasbrouck, J. & Tindal, G. (2006) "Oral Reading Fluency Norms: A valuable assessment tool for reading teachers" *The Reading Teacher,* 59(7), 636–644.

Hoyt, L. (2008) *Revisit, Reflect, Retell: Time-tested Strategies for Teaching Reading Comprehension.* Portsmouth, NH: Heinemann.

Jamison Rog, L. (2010) *Marvelous Minilessons for Teaching Intermediate Writing, Grades 3–6.* Newark, DE: International Reading Association.

Jamison Rog, L. (2012) *Guiding Readers: Making the Most of the 18-minute Guided Reading Lesson.* Markham, ON: Pembroke.

Keene, E. & Zimmerman, S. (2007) *Mosaic of Thought (2nd Edition).* Portland, ME: Stenhouse.

Kissner, E. (2006) *Summarizing, Paraphrasing and Retelling: Skills for Better Reading, Writing and Test Taking.* Portsmouth, NH: Heinemann.

Klingner, J. & Vaughn, S. (1998) "Teaching Reading Comprehension through Collaborative Strategic Reading" *Intervention in School and Clinic,* May 1999, vol. 34, no. 5, 284–292.

Lyman, F. (1981) "The Responsive Classroom Discussion: The inclusion of all students" *Mainstreaming Digest.* College Park, MD: University of Maryland.

Martinez, M., Roser, N. & Strecker, S. (1999) "'I never thought I could be a star!' A readers theatre ticket to fluency" *The Reading Teacher,* 53, 326–334.

Marzano, R., Pickering, D. & Pollock, J. (2001) *Classroom Instruction That Works: Research-Based Strategies for Increasing Student Achievement.* Alexandria, VA: ASCD.

McGregor, T. (2007) *Comprehension Connections.* Portsmouth, NH: Heinemann.

McKeown, M., Beck, I. & Blake, R. (2009) "Rethinking Reading Comprehension Instruction: A comparison of instruction for strategies and content approaches" *Reading Research Quarterly,* 44:3 (July/August/September 2009), 218–255.

Moore, D. & Readence, J.E. (1984) "A Quantitative and Qualitative Review of Graphic Organizer Research" *Journal of Educational Research,* 78(1), 11–17.

Nagy, W.E., & Anderson, R.C. (1984) "How Many Words Are There in Printed School English?" *Reading Research Quarterly,* 19, 304–330.

Nagy, W., Anderson, R. & Herman, P. (1987) "Learning Word Meanings from Context During Normal Reading" *American Educational Research Journal,* 24, 237–270.

National Reading Panel (2000) *Teaching Children to Read (Report of the Subgroups).* Washington, DC: U.S. Department of Health and Human Services.

Nystrand, M. (1999) "The Contexts of Learning: Foundations of academic achievement" *English Update: A Newsletter From the Center on English Learning and Achievement,* Spring 1999: 2, 8.

Nystrand, M., Wu, L. L. Gamoran, A., Zeiser, S. & Long, D. A. (2003) "Questions in Time: Investigating the structure and dynamics of unfolding classroom discourse" *Discourse Processes,* 35(2), 135–196.

Ogle, D. (1986) "K-W-L: A teaching model that develops active reading of expository text" *The Reading Teacher,* 39, 564–70.

Ontario Ministry of Education (2008) *A Guide to Effective Literacy Instruction, Grades 4-6, Volume 6: Writing.* Toronto, ON.

Opitz, M.F. & Rasinski, T.V. (1998) *Good-bye Round Robin: 25 Effective Oral Reading Strategies.* Portsmouth, NH: Heinemann.

Pearson, P.D. (2013) "Research Foundations of the Common Core State Standards in English Language Arts" in S. Newman and L. Gambrell (Eds.) *Quality Reading Instruction in the Age of Common Core State Standards.* Newark, DE: International Reading Association.

Raphael, T., Highfield, K. & Au, K. (2006) *QAR Now.* New York, NY: Scholastic.

Rasinski, T.M. (2000) "Speed Does Matter in Reading" *The Reading Teacher* 54, 146–151.

Reutzel, R., Jones, C., Fawson, P. & Smith, J. (2008) "Scaffolded Silent Reading: A complement to guided repeated oral reading that works!" *The Reading Teacher*, 62:3 Nov. 194–207.

Roberts, G., Vaughn, S., Fletcher, J., Stuebing, K. & Barth, A. (2013) "Effects of a Response-based, Tiered Framework for Intervening with Struggling Readers in Middle School" *Reading Research Quarterly*, 48:3, July/August/September.

Rowe, M.B. (1986) "Wait Time: Slowing down may be a way of speeding up!" *Journal of Teacher Education*, 37:43.

Schumm, J.S., Moody, S.W. & Vaughn, S. (2000) "Grouping for Reading Instruction: Does one size fit all?" *Journal of Learning Disabilities*, 33(5), 477-488.

Schwartz, S., & Bone, M. (1995) *Retelling, Relating, Reflecting: Beyond the 3 R's.* Toronto, ON: NelsonThomson Learning.

Smith, F., Hardman, F., Wall, K. & Mroz, M. (2004) "Interactive Whole Class Teaching in the National Literacy and Numeracy Strategies" *British Educational Research Journal*, 30 (3), 395–411.

Stahl, S.A. (1999) *Vocabulary Development.* Cambridge, MA: Brookline Books.

Stanovich, K.E. (1986) "Matthew Effects in Reading: Some consequences of individual differences in the acquisition of literacy" *Reading Research Quarterly*, 22, 360–407.

Stead, T. (2005) *Reality Checks: Teaching Comprehension with Nonfiction Texts, K–8.* Portland, ME: Stenhouse.

Therrien, W. (2004) "Fluency and Comprehension Gains as a Result of Repeated Reading: A meta-analysis" *Remedial and Special Education* July/August; 25:4; 252–261.

Therrien, W. &. Kubina, R. (2006) "Developing Reading Fluency with Repeated Reading" *Intervention in School and Clinic* Vol. 41, No. 3, January.

Torgesen, J.K., Houston, D.D., Rissman, L.M., Decker, S.M., Roberts, G., Vaughn, S., Wexler, J. Francis, D.J, Rivera, M.O. & Lesaux, N. (2007) *Academic Literacy Instruction for Adolescents: A guidance document from the Center on Instruction.* Portsmouth, NH: RMC Research Corporation, Center on Instruction.

Trotter, A. (2007) "Federal Study Finds No Edge for Students Using Technology-Based Reading and Math Products" *Education Week*, April 4, 2007.

Vaughn, S., Chard, D., Pedrotty Bryant, D., Coleman, M., Tyler, B. & Thompson, S. (2000) "Fluency and Comprehension Interventions for Third-grade Students" *Remedial and Special Education*, 21, 325–335.

Weinreich, H., Obendorf, H., Herder, E. & Mayer, M. (2008) "Not Quite the Average: An empirical study of web use" *ACM Transactions on the Web* 2:1 (February), article #5.

Zygouris-Coe, V. (2012) "Eyes on Disciplinary Literacy" *Reading Today Online*. International Reading Association http://www.reading.org/general/publications/blog/BlogSinglePost/12-07-24/Eyes_on_Disciplinary_Literacy.aspx#. Ul_6ZBClCpo

Texts Used for Samples

Asselstine, Les & Peturson, Rod, *Science Everywhere Grade* 5 (Harcourt Canada, 1999)

Brown, Liz, *The Bully* (HIP, 2005)

Brown, Margaret Wise, *The Important Book* (Harper Collins, 1999)

Fleischman, Paul, *Big Talk: Poems for Four Voices* (Candlewick, 2000)

Fleischman, Paul, *I Am Phoenix: Poems for Two Voices* (HarperTrophy, 1989)

Fleischman, Paul, *Joyful Noise: Poems for Two Voices* (HarperTrophy, 1992)

Jacobson, Sid & Ernie Colon, *Anne Frank: The Anne Frank House Authorized Biography* (Hill and Wang, 2010)

Jamison, Lori, *Frozen* (HIP, 2012)

Jennings, Sharon, *Baseball Bats* (HIP, 2011)

Kropp, Paul, *Caught in the Blizzard* (HIP, 2003)

Kropp, Paul, *The Crash* (HIP, 2005)

Kropp, Paul, *Ghost House* (HIP, 2003)

McNicoll, Sylvia, *Dog on Trial* (HIP, 2013)

O'Neill, Mary, *Hailstones and Halibut Bones* (Doubleday, 1961)

Rowling, J.K., *Harry Potter and the Philosopher's Stone* (Bloomsbury Publishing, 1997)

van Allsburg, Chris, *The Mysteries of Harris Burdick* (Houghton-Mifflin, 1984)

van Allsburg, Chris, *The Chronicles of Harris Burdick: Fourteen Amazing Authors Tell the Tales* (Houghton-Mifflin, 2011)

Index